THORNTON WILDER

Modern Literature Monographs

THORNTON WILDER

Hermann Stresau

Translated by Frieda Schutze

Frederick Ungar Publishing Co.
New York

Translated from the original German and published by
arrangement with Colloquium Verlag, Berlin

Copyright © 1971 by
Frederick Ungar Publishing Co., Inc.
Printed in the United States of America
Library of Congress Catalog Card Number: 71-149478
ISBN: 0-8044-2844-1 (cloth)
        0-8044-6884-2 (paper)

Contents

1

Anonymous,
but Not
Impersonal

In its biographical facts, Thornton Wilder's life is distinguished from that of many of his literary compatriots by its rather unadventurous stability and normality: in his youth he was neither a hobo nor a dishwasher, neither a cotton picker nor a stevedore. Nor did he, like Sherwood Anderson, abruptly give up the management of a factory in order to devote himself to literature. And although his father owned and published a newspaper, Wilder was not even a journalist, an occupation that has often been a preliminary stage in the development of a number of successful authors.

Wilder has had the typical career of an academically trained school and university teacher. It is difficult to determine which is his greater passion: teaching—the pedagogic relationship with young people —or the art of writing. He undoubtedly owes his extraordinary teaching ability and his writing style to his unconventional liveliness. This manner has been described repeatedly and consistently by those who have seen and spoken with him. A German student who made his acquaintance in 1952 at Harvard wrote:

Suddenly changing from his customary deep, warm voice to a surprisingly high treble, he repeats what is to him the decisive, final word two or three times, like a waterfall, almost in a singing tone. . . . The longer you are in his company the more clearly you recognize the passionate teacher wholeheartedly dedicated to his task, the more definitely does the author or even the poet you thought you were going to meet recede into the background. . . . To judge from his casual clothes—loose tie and unpressed trousers—one could take him for a businessman, a salesman.

His German translator Hans Sahl (*Perspektiven* 8, 1954), on the other hand, speaks of a certain Spanish *grandezza,*

which, with his hat pulled down at an angle over his face, gives him an almost bold and challenging aspect. . . . It was the unusual in his otherwise very usual appearance—the cultivation and refinement, so to speak, of a normal type common in this country—which at once distinguished him from this normal type and added a new element to the striking, almost scholarly distinction of his bearing.

It is this combination *grandezza* and a friendly courteousness that characterizes his behavior toward people.

In Wilder one will seek in vain for the problems of the "lost generation" of the 1920s, of Hemingway, Fitzgerald, and Dos Passos—expatriates (excepting Dos Passos) who became disillusioned, by World War I, in American values. These were young men upon whom the war had inflicted a deep shock that they were able to overcome in literature—or that, perhaps, enhanced their writing—if not altogether in life. And yet it is to their generation that Wilder belongs.

Thornton Wilder was born on 17 April 1897 in Madison, Wisconsin. Thus, like Hemingway (born in 1899), Fitzgerald (born in 1896), and Dos Passos (born in 1896), he was a child of the Middle West. His father was Amos P. Wilder, and his mother was Isabel Niven Wilder, the daughter of a Presbyterian minister in New York. Thornton grew up in a puri-

tanical environment. His first school years were spent
in Madison. Then, during the era of Theodore Roose-
velt, his father, who was an enthusiastic supporter of
the President, was sent as consul general to Hong
Kong. He was later sent to Shanghai where Thornton
attended a mission school for six months. In 1906,
Mrs. Wilder brought her five children to California
for their education, and from 1911 to 1912 they lived
again in China, where Thornton attended a German
and an English mission school. Returning to California, Thornton graduated from Berkeley High School
in 1915. He spent the next two years at Oberlin College in Ohio, and from 1917 to 1918 he attended Yale
University, where he studied modern languages and
published essays and short plays in the *Yale University Magazine.*

When the United States entered World War I,
Wilder volunteered several times, but was rejected
because of his eyesight. He was finally accepted in
the coast artillery where he became a sergeant, serving eight months without leaving the country. In
World War II, Wilder served from 1942 until December 1945 in a more dangerous capacity. Already an
established author, he became a captain and then a
lieutenant colonel in the Army Air Corps, serving in
Africa and Italy. Despite the obvious dangers of war-
time service, he was able to see a very positive side to
the experience. "I have always felt," he said in a conversation with Richard H. Goldstone, "that both en-
listments were valuable to me for a number of rea-

sons,"[1] the chief one being that the soldier's life kept him from

being almost exclusively thrown in with persons more or less in the arts. . . . One of the benefits of military serv ice . . . is being thrown into daily contact with non-artists, something a young American writer should consciously seek.[2]

Wilder sees a great danger for the American artist who lives only with his own kind. He spoke emphatically about the danger of "introversion," perhaps on the basis of his own experience.

But in general Wilder does not care to talk about himself. "I thought we were supposed to talk about the art of the novel," he said in the interview with Goldstone.[3] Although he readily answers the question as to what made him want to write, he does so in such a general and indirect manner that his own personality is almost entirely effaced. He reveals little except what pertains to the business of being a writer or his youthful feeling about language:

For a long time I tried to explain to myself the spell of Madame de Sévigné; she is not devastatingly witty nor wise. She is simply at one with French syntax. Phrase, sentence, and paragraph breathe this effortless at-home-ness with how one sees, feels, and says a thing in the French language . . . she had merely to exhibit the genius in the language.[4]

The creative impulse was at work in Thornton at an early age. Of his childhood it is known that, even as a ten-year-old, he read a great deal and played

imaginative games with his brother and sisters. The
plays he wrote and staged as a boy with his brother
(who later became professor of theology) and his sisters foreshadowed the three-minute plays that he later
wrote as a student and a young teacher.

Wilder says that his childhood was not unhappy.
Nonetheless, puritanical upbringing often results in
great introspection. In the Goldstone interview he
said:

I have never been unoccupied. That's as near as I can get
to a statement about the happiness or unhappiness of my
childhood. Yet I am convinced that, except in a few extraordinary cases, one form or another of an unhappy
childhood is essential to the formation of exceptional
gifts. Perhaps I should have been a better man if I had
had an unequivocally unhappy childhood.[5]

It is possible that the early years spent away from
America encouraged in him very different tendencies
from those of the "lost generation." His great interest
in classical languages and classical poetry soon became evident. Among Wilder's gifts there is a sort of
deep, well-balanced objectivity that, though probably
muffled in his early youth by an extravagant imagination, led him to be inclined to accept the world as
it was and, at the same time, to develop a sense of the
inadequacies of human nature.

Wilder's habit of giving only scant information
about himself has kept him almost anonymous as a
person, and the remaining biographical data may be
briefly summarized. He graduated from Yale Univer-

sity in 1920, that same year published his first drama, *The Trumpet Shall Sound*, in the *Yale University Magazine*, and spent the year 1920–1921 studying archaeology at the American Academy in Rome. From 1921 until 1928 he taught French in a school at Lawrenceville, New Jersey, while continuing his French studies at Princeton. He received his master's degree in 1925. During this period, he took a year for travel, again in Europe, before returning to Lawrenceville. *The Cabala* appeared in 1926. In 1927 he published *The Bridge of San Luis Rey*, which won the Pulitzer Prize and soon became a great success. This led to the publication of the early short plays under the title *The Angel That Troubled the Waters* (1928), and the novel *The Woman of Andros* (1930). A volume of one-act plays entitled *The Long Christmas Dinner* appeared in 1931.

For six years Wilder lectured on comparative literature at the University of Chicago. During the summer holidays he undertook lecture tours or worked for a few weeks in Hollywood film studios, translated and adapted *Le Viol de Lucrèce* by André Obey, adapted *A Doll's House* by Henrik Ibsen, delivered guest lectures at the University of Hawaii, and acted as American delegate to the Paris Institut de Cooperation Intellectuelle. His novel *Heaven's My Destination* appeared in 1935. In 1938 his play *Our Town*, which had been produced without much success in Princeton and Boston, was a success on Broadway and won for him a second Pulitzer Prize. In 1939 the farce

The Merchant of Yonkers appeared, having been directed the year before by Max Reinhardt in New York.

In October 1942, *The Skin of Our Teeth* was first performed in New Haven, Connecticut, and thereafter was produced in several American theaters and in London. *The Ides of March* was published in 1948. At the 1949 Goethe celebration in Aspen, Colorado, Wilder gave the principal address. In 1950–51 he taught at Harvard, and in 1952 he headed the American delegation to the UNESCO conference in Venice. A later version of *The Merchant of Yonkers*, entitled *The Matchmaker*, was produced in 1955 at the Edinburgh Festival where, at the same time, "Alcestiad" was staged under the title "A Life in the Sun." In 1961 "The Long Christmas Dinner," set to music by Paul Hindemith and translated into German, was produced in Mannheim, Germany, and in 1962 "The Alcestiad" was produced as an opera by Louise Talma in Frankfurt-on-the-Main. From two cycles of seven short dramas, *The Seven Deadly Sins* and *The Seven Ages of Man*, three short plays were produced in New York in 1962.

In the spring of 1962 Wilder retired to the Arizona desert for two years, in order to work out old plans, undistracted by travel or literary commitments.

In literature Wilder has respected highly such avant-garde figures as Ezra Pound, Gertrude Stein (whom he met in Chicago), and James Joyce, maintaining that he was influenced by them. In his Preface to *Three Plays*, Wilder writes about *The Skin of Our*

Teeth: "The play is deeply indebted to James Joyce's
Finnegans Wake. I should be very happy if, in the
future, some author should feel similarly indebted to
any work of mine."[6]

This admiration doubtlessly applied largely to the
standards, the unequivocal, undeviating aspirations
of those innovators, for Wilder's own work shows an
insistence upon a rigid standard. His comment about
Madame de Sévigné reveals something of the superior
demands of the artist whose instinct is directed toward
the greatest possible mastery of his medium of expression.

Guided by such ideals and by his innate and ac-
quired thoroughness, Wilder made many literary and
musical treasures of world culture his own. Next to
writing, music remains his favorite occupation, his
talents extending even to composition. He once said
that he would like to live to be one hundred and fifty
in order to become proficient in many more fields.

Wilder has received various honorary doctorates
and memberships. Among them are those awarded
by the universities of New York, Yale, Harvard,
Oberlin, Frankfurt-on-the-Main, and Zurich. He was
also awarded the Goethe Plaque and a gold medal
from the American Academy of Art and Literature,
of which he is a member. In 1957 the Peace Medal of
Pour le Merité was awarded him by the President of
the German Federal Republic.

The recognition that Wilder received did not lure
him into unrestrained productivity. Even his "long"
works, the novels and dramas, are not very extensive.

In terms of sheer bulk, his entire published work is relatively little. In the conversation with Richard H. Goldstone, when Wilder was asked why he wrote, he replied ironically: "I think I write in order to discover on my shelf a new book which I would enjoy reading."[7] Asked whether his books fulfilled this expectation, he said no and added that a writer, after all, cannot experience the sensation of reading one of his own books as though he had never read it before. "Yet with each new work that expectation is prompting me."[8] "Unfortunately," he said, "good things are not made by the resolve to make a good thing, but by the application to develop fitly the one specific idea or project that presents itself to you."[9] With this, Wilder touched on the most precarious problem of writing, for who is going to tell the author that he is really "developing fitly" the subject that presents itself to him? Wilder mentions that he started many such experiments and discarded them. "The decision to abandon [a work] is hard."[10] There are actually no fragments that he considered worthy of publication. From this one can draw a number of conclusions about Wilder's conscientiousness. And one may also surmise that during the years of writing there must have been many "projects" that presented themselves to him.

Wilder has pointed out the dangers of success, which, according to him, are as great as those of nonsuccess. From his advice to young authors one may conclude that he himself knew how to avoid those dangers. He recommended keeping a diary, not for publication, but for the sake of "inner concentration."

He advised young writers to discipline themselves and learn from the master, whereupon originality would come of itself. He warned against trying to achieve originality at any price. One should write, he says, only on subjects that one commands. "I consider it best to write about things that lie on the boundaries of the unknown." A writer should be proud of his solitude and concentrate wholly upon his subject, regardless of the public, of friends, even of his own hopes. This and the warning against introversion mentioned earlier may explain why Wilder's work has remained relatively scant. It is, in fact, the product of great concentration.

At first it may seem that Wilder's writing contradicts his own recommendation, since it deals to a certain extent with events that undoubtedly lie outside his realm of personal experience. However, in exotic objects and themes he may have found elements of human existence that have a universal validity and that confront the living individual with problems that recur in every age. Seen from this point of view, periods of time do not appear as closed entities.

His journeys in North and South America and on the European continent, as well as his varied connections and functions, have kept Wilder's mind open to the world, the old and the new. Thornton Wilder, the American—for despite his cosmopolitanism, he is definitely an American—is attracted to Europe apparently because this ancient continent, with all its upheavals, has kept a deeply rooted, richly diversified, and somehow instructive tradition. This tradition, with its fusion of antiquity and Christianity, could, as Wilder sees it, once again become more meaningful even to the European.

Yet Wilder remains free of all romanticism; he does not glorify the past at the expense of the present. This is implied in the address he gave in 1957 when he was awarded the prestigious Peace Prize of the German publishers. On this occasion he pointed out the danger inherent in past cultures that had been sustained by an elite, as well as the danger posed by a culture of masses of individuals with equal rights, one that we are inevitably, but in the end fortunately, faced with. Americans, he maintained, unlike Europeans, do not really know who they are—a surprisingly independent dictum in view of the popular, almost dogmatic insistence on the American way of life. He emphasized, however, that Americans are nevertheless committed to the task of developing a new human being whose chief characteristic is to regard every other individual as made of the same human stuff. Since every individual is merely one among millions, the American is "friendly" to all, not out of goodness, condescension, or conceit, but because he realizes that every human being must be free to choose how to live his own life, without help from anyone. This attitude may not be characteristic of all Americans, but surely it is characteristic of Wilder.

2

The Cabala

The Cabala (1926) goes back to Wilder's sojourn in Rome and therefore has a slight autobiographical foundation. Although the story is told in the first person, however, the autobiographical references have been concealed to the point of unrecognizability, and it is quite improbable that the young Wilder experienced the events as he describes them.

The title is reminiscent of Jewish mysticism or of the English secret society during the reign of Charles II in the seventeenth century. The story deals with a variety of plots, intrigues, and society gossip among a rather loosely joined group composed of wealthy, extremely conservative individuals—some of aristocratic backgrounds—living in modern Rome. Unable to adjust to modern political realities—the growing threat of fascism is mentioned occasionally —they cultivate ideas of a peculiarly retrogressive, highly reactionary utopia. The narrator's informant, an American archaeologist named James Blair, who introduces his young compatriot to the circle, describes it somewhat disdainfully as an "international set" made up chiefly of women, a hothouse of inbred human beings who live in a perpetual dream. Occasionally they have a mild influence on politics, thanks to their social connections, but this is so insignificant that it is only hinted at in passing. The clique is held together by the vague concept of a semimystical, hierarchic-royalistic order to be introduced by the Church.

Wilder is obviously less interested in the history of the Cabala than in the character and fate of its individual members. Without exception they are cases of human existence on the borderline between reality and nonreality. Yet in the very marginal nature of their lives they reveal crises of the spirit that transcend the banal, the practical, and the purely factual. Even the archaeologist Blair is a marginal figure, though he does not belong to the Cabala and is quite indifferent to its ideology. He is a scholar, but there is something strange about his scholarship: he constantly searches out facts and fills whole volumes with notes, without ever bringing these facts into any kind of relationship. Although he moves within reality, it is a chaotic reality.

The members of the Cabala, on the other hand, like rare creatures in an aquarium, move in nonreality. One and all, they seem to be living in an artificial light: Miss Grier, the leader of the circle; the Duchess d'Aquilanera, who is greatly troubled about her unstable son, Marcantonio; Alix, the capricious, gifted, but deeply unhappy Princess d'Espoli, who is hopelessly in love with James Blair; Astrée-Luce de Morfontaine, who is consumed with religious hysteria; and, finally, the strangest and most important figure of all, Cardinal Vaini.

The novel actually consists of separate tales depicting the fate of each of these figures and their relationships to one another. There is a certain vacillation, a slight uncertainty in the grouping of motifs and in the entire subject matter. One incident appears as a harsh dissonance in the unity of the whole—and, strangely enough, it appears at the very beginning, before the individual stories. Blair and his friend visit a dying English poet, who begs the archaeologist to remind the painter who is nursing him that there must be no name on his grave. "Just write: 'Here lies one whose name was writ in water.' "[1] This statement and the rest of the circumstances—the painter's initials *F.S.*, the sick man's comment that he had studied to be a doctor, even the proximity to the Piazza di Spagna, as well as the narrator's concluding statement that, immediately following his death, the poet's fame "had begun to spread over the whole world"—all definitely point to the English poet John Keats. The episode has no sequel, it is never mentioned again. But since the first part of the narration —the more general introduction to the Cabala group —is written in an ironical key that subsequently gives place to a warmer note, it is not inconceivable that the plan of the whole was originally different and that the "Keats" episode had a somewhat different significance.

Superficially, the Keats figure serves as contrast: the poet is dying, but his short life was to have an immortal success. The Cabala circle as a whole, however, along with its individual members, seems condemned to hopeless failure. The Keats figure also represents a sacrifice, just as those Cabalists whose fate the narrator depicts are sacrifices. There are other contrasting figures, such as the American traveler Perkins with his naïve officiousness or the Latin teacher from Grand Rapids "who had come over to put her hand on the Forum." Finally, the narrator himself is a decided contrasting figure. As the modern Puritan, he moves among the eccentric royalists who treat him partly as an amusing diversion, partly as a trusted messenger and mediator, often as a friend and mentor.

In the last capacity, however, his efforts are futile. Marcantonio with all his ridiculous, meaningless titles; the Princess d'Espoli with her unrequited love (a recurring theme in many of Wilder's works); the devout, but too unworldly and naïve Astrée-Luce de Morfontaine—all of them founder, as does the most significant figure of this unrealistic circle, the very clever Cardinal, who has lost his simple faith.

Once, the Cardinal's faith had taken him to China as a missionary, but he returned a skeptical old man, skeptical even of religious testimonies. He doubts that it is possible to prove the existence of God. Three of his statements, especially, remain in one's memory: "Who can understand literature unless he has suffered? Who can understand religion unless he has sinned? Who can understand love unless he has loved without response?"[2]

Hoping to escape despair, the Cardinal sets out once more for the land of his greatest triumph. He dies on the journey and is buried at sea. Thus, his name truly becomes "writ in water."

It is a twilight of the gods that is symbolically depicted here. Miss Grier, the leader of the group, is the one who finally speaks of it. The gods, the natural enemies of Christianity, "in whose presence every man is a failure," finally give in; "they go over [to the enemy]."[3]

On a clear, starlit night, Virgil, the spirit of the West, the mediator between antiquity and Christianity, appears to the narrator aboard a ship returning to his American home. "Seek out some city that is young," he says. "The secret is to make a city, not to rest in it. When you have found one, drink in the illusion that she too is eternal."[4] Rome, he continues, was great. He, Virgil, cannot enter Zion until he has forgotten Rome—but he cannot forget Rome. In the new world a new Rome awaits its greatness.

This is the underlying motif of *The Cabala*. As a young man, the narrator had a map of Rome hanging above his desk, and, longingly, he studied the plan of the Eternal City. Now, having come to the city, he recognizes instead "human ruins," and it is these he describes. And finally, he returns to the new world which, compared to Europe, is still "new." It is the Henry James theme of the relationship between America and the old world. The twilight of the gods has settled over the old world, but in it appears the image of Virgil, the great exemplar. It is as though this Roman could, to some extent, invest the almost ridiculous inadequacies of the Cabalists with a humanity that lends warmth and beauty even to the decay.

3

The Bridge of
San Luis Rey

In an essay on James Joyce, Wilder wrote that an author continually searches for the theme or subject he can call his own, for a great mythical theme that is awaiting only his discovery of it—his "Gulliver and his Robinson Crusoe."

In his search for a subject matter of his own, Wilder came across Prosper Mérimée's drama *La Carosse du Saint-Sacrement* (1829), a play about the famous actress Camila Perichole that takes place in Lima, Peru. Camila, the mistress of the viceroy, extorts from the latter the gift of a luxury coach such as even very few noblemen could command. She enjoys her triumph, but then, in a sudden change of heart, she presents the coach to the church, so that the priests, when they set out to administer extreme unction to the dying, need no longer travel on foot. This play gave Wilder the idea for *The Bridge of San Luis Rey*. The figure of Camila Perichole (who, incidentally, is an historical figure, though Wilder placed her in a period several decades before she actually lived) plays a significant role in the book.

This novel, which was awarded the Pulitzer Prize, was extraordinarily successful. Perhaps its success can be attributed to the unusual amalgamation of European classical elements with an American naturalness of form. Or perhaps it was the unusual subject matter. It was probably both and, not least, the mastery with which the various elements were woven together into a unity.

The story begins quite simply and factually: "On Friday noon, July the twentieth, 1714, the finest

bridge in all Peru broke and precipitated five travel-
lers into the gulf below."[1] A much-used suspension
bridge, it was woven of osiers in Inca times and was
considered indestructible. This awesome event is the
core of the three stories that make up the novel. The
arrangement and interrelation of these, as in *The
Cabala*, form variations on a central theme.

Again Wilder introduces an outside figure who
is not directly involved with the victims. He is
Brother Juniper, a rational theologian, who believes
that this catastrophe has finally offered to him a sci-
entifically valid vehicle that will enable him to prove
the existence of a Divine Providence and its justness.
He ends up with a comprehensive book, a vast collection of material that he has assembled through years
of effort. On the basis of countless facts about the
lives of the victims, he tries unsuccessfully to arrive
at a system that is meant to prove God's justice. But
his efforts are declared heretical and Brother Juniper,
along with his book, is condemned and burned by the
Inquisition in the village square of Puerto.

In unfolding the histories of the victims, the narrator is concerned not with their external fates but
with the internal processes that Brother Juniper's
facts cannot convey. Here are the stories of the Marquesa de Montemayor and her young companion,
Pepita; of the twin brothers Esteban and Manuel;
and of Uncle Pio. Interwoven with these are the
stories of the actress Camila Perichole; the Abbess
María del Pilar; and the Marquesa's daughter, the
Condesa Clara d'Abuirre, the recipient of many ma-

ternal letters that one day are to become famous for
their classical Spanish style.

In her grief over her unloving daughter, married
in distant Spain, the old, ugly Marquesa had become
sadly negligent of herself. She had been drinking
heavily and had fallen from her traditional religion
into a primitive superstition. While on a pilgrimage,
shortly before the accident puts an end to her life,
a tide of resignation sweeps over her. The change
comes when, seeing her sleeping companion, Pepita,
who in all innocence and selflessness has remained
faithful to her, she renounces her own selfish love for
her daughter: "Tomorrow I begin a new life. . . ."
She is never put to the test.

The second story tells of the fates of the twin
brothers Esteban and Manuel, who, reared as foundlings in the convent of Madre María del Pilar, are so
inseparably one that they cannot be distinguished.
They even speak a language they contrived, which
no one else can understand. When Manuel falls pas-
sionately in love with the Perichole, the close relationship of the brothers is destroyed. Not long after,
Manuel accidently cuts his knee and dies from the
wound. Esteban, left alone after the untimely death
of his brother, wanders restlessly about the country-
side. Captain Alvarado, a friend of María del Pilar,
prevents him at the last moment from committing
suicide. It is shortly after this that he crosses the
bridge and meets his death. To Captain Alvarado,
who understands loneliness well, Esteban had

shouted: "I am alone, alone, alone."[2] Death releases him from his loneliness.

The victims of the catastrophe in the third story are Uncle Pio and the Perichole's son, Don Jaime. Uncle Pio had once been the friend and confidant, the somewhat suspect guardian and tutor, of Camila Perichole. The Marquesa had once written to her daughter that no one knew whether Uncle Pio was Camila's lover, her father, or her son. Perhaps Uncle Pio, who taught Camila her art and then lost his beloved because his teaching had been too successful, was the true artist. As the celebrated actress and interpreter of Calderón and the mistress of the viceroy, Camila had outgrown Uncle Pio. And yet he still loved her.

"Just give me up," she tells him when he seeks her out on her country estate. "Just put me out of your mind."[3] She does not want to hear about the past. "A great pain lay at her heart, the pain of a world that was meaningless."[4] However, she permits Uncle Pio, a dedicated teacher, to take her son in order to educate him. On their way to the capital, the bridge collapses and Uncle Pio and the boy die.

Camila, who is not one of those killed, plays an important part in all the stories. She is the axis, as it were, around which everything turns. She appears first in the story of the Marquesa de Montemayor, who, in order to gather new material for her letters to her daughter, visits the theater one evening with Pepita. Camila Perichole is playing one of her best

roles. In an entr'acte she improvises couplets ridicul-
ing the grotesque woman who, sitting in her box lost
in thought, is unaware of what is taking place. Pepita
whispers to her that they should go, and as they leave
the box, the house bursts "into a roar of triumph."

The enraged viceroy insists that Camila apolo-
gize. She calls upon the Marquesa and is overcome
by the realization that the old woman, drunk as
usual, knows nothing of the scandal. In grotesquely
humble admiration, the Marquesa begs the actress
to forgive her for leaving the theater before the end
of the performance. Camila Perichole is moved by
the dignity, indeed the nobility of the old woman:
"When she was drunk she wore the grandeur of
Hecuba."[5] Filled with shame, she returns home in
consternation.

Camila Perichole is the woman who indirectly
causes Manuel's death by destroying his will to live,
and who indirectly causes Esteban's deep unhappiness. And in the life of Uncle Pio, as we have seen,
the actress plays the chief and fateful role. At the end
of the novel, Camila even enters into the life of the
Abbess María del Pilar, to whose convent she comes
after long seclusion.

The reader may be struck by the fact that few
of the characters have strong family ties. The Marquesa, to be sure, is a mother. Indeed, she is a mother
first of all. But she had become one by an unloved
husband whom she was forced by her family to
marry. An ocean now separates her from her child,
and she remains unloved and lonely. Pepita is an

orphan. The twin brothers are foundlings. Uncle Pio, though he came from a good Castilian house, was illegitimate and left home when he was a boy to make his way as an adventurer. The Abbess María del Pilar is a nun living outside family relationships. And by his very profession Captain Alvarado, whose beloved daughter had died several years before, is left to his own resources. This solitariness could, perhaps, have occurred as a theme only to a modern American. Again most of the characters live on the borderline between the real and the nonreal, though their cases, certainly, are not as extreme as those of *The Cabala*.

Whereas *The Cabala* deals with very strange and even abstruse ideas, with women whose hysteria verges on psychosis, the characters of this novel are isolated, but comparatively normal, human beings. Their fate is not bound up with an ideology, but with something universally human—the inadequacy of striving. Wilder seems to imply that even the family offers no protection against this inadequacy: "She [the Marquesa] secretly refused to believe that any-one (herself excepted) loved anyone. All families lived in a wasteful atmosphere of custom and kissed one another with secret indifference."[6]

From the point of view of the temporal life of man, there is a definitely pessimistic strain running through the novel. This is contrapuntally offset by a religiosity that is vague and casual and by an unsen-timental, slightly ironical imperturbability in the storytelling. One reason for the success of the novel is the steady calm with which disturbing, even excit-

ing events are related—events that show man's de-
fenselessness, the suffocating meaninglessness of existence, the cold loneliness of the individual, and at
the same time his deep longing for security, love, and
meaningfulness.

In contrast to *The Cabala*, there is a more rigid
form, a clearer composition, resulting from the greater
aloofness of an omniscient narrator.

The reader is also likely to be impressed by descriptions of some very lovely moments. He is not
offered many such pictures, but their very paucity
makes them more telling. One example is the terse
description of the landscape when, shortly before he
witnesses the accident, Brother Juniper sees the
snowy peaks of the Andes and remembers the biblical
words about the mountains from whence "help
cometh." Or the old Marquesa, on the night before
her death, looking at "the stars that glittered above
the Andes. Throughout the hours of the night, though
there had been few to hear it, the whole sky had been
loud with the singing of these constellations."[7]

The brief description of the air, mountains, and
stars seen from the pilgrimage town of Cluxambuqua
evokes a vision of the awe-inspiring vastness of eternal and immovable nature in contrast to the pettiness
of human destinies.

4

Three-Minute

Plays

The art of the first two novels, oriented in the tradition of the West, yet not weakened by romantic sentimentalism, might have been in danger of petrifying had not Wilder, with his "three-minute" plays, found his own form to express the things he had to say. The brevity in form of the plays in *The Angel That Troubled the Waters* (1928) seems to be characteristic for Wilder. Even when young, Wilder was aware of unnecessary repetition and the smug complacency of so much that is written. Within the "three-minute" plays, he claims to have found the form that could satisfy his desire for brevity and compactness. He has even humorously stated that, plagued by an "inertia that barely permits me to write at all," this form flatters his inability to sustain long flights.

The passion for brevity was already evident in the novels, which contained only what was absolutely essential: mere scenery was kept from having a diverting or digressing effect. Wilder would seem to agree with Ernest Hemingway's statement that prose is architecture, not interior decoration. Even *Heaven's My Destination*, which followed in 1935, was similarly constructed; it contains more dialogue than description.

The idea of writing "three-minute" plays goes back to Wilder's school days. The flyleaves of an old algebra book contained a list of titles that he drew up in Berkeley, California, in the spring of 1915. Many of them remained unwritten. The very titles suggest exotic contents: "The Angel on the Ship," "And the

Sea Shall Give Up Its Dead," "Now the Servant's Name Was Malchus," "The Angel That Troubled the Waters"—to name only a few. Wilder maintains that he wrote these plays to be read, not to be performed.

The "three-minute" play entitled "Mozart and the Grey Steward" begins quite realistically, with Mozart writing the orchestration for *The Magic Flute*. The masked steward of Count von Walsegg arrives and commissions the *Requiem* for his master. In a dream, however, the Grey Steward returns, and this time it is Death. " 'Know first,' " he says, " 'that all the combinations of circumstances can suffer two interpretations, the apparent and the real.' "[1] Mozart, he goes on to say, should " 'give a voice to all those millions sleeping, who have no one but you to speak for them. . . . Only through the intercession of great love, and of great art which is love, can that despairing cry be eased. Was that not sufficient cause for this commission to be anonymous?' "[2] (Incidentally, we see here the reason Wilder has always avoided biographical questions: the passage just quoted is a wishful image, and Wilder's love of music has clothed it in this form.)

The transition from the real to surrealism occurs without any mysterious preliminary indications, and Death identifies himself in matter-of-fact words. There is no doubt, however, that Death and what he says belong to the sphere of the "real." It is in this sphere of the real, which lies behind or within actuality, that most of the "three-minute" plays are en-

tirely or partially set. This is true of "Nascuntur
Poetae," of "Leviathan," of "Flight into Egypt," and
of "Centaurs."

In "Centaurs" the English poet Shelley steps in
front of the curtain while the audience is assembling
for a performance of Ibsen's *The Master Builder*.
Somewhat timidly Shelley announces that he con-
ceived the play, but that death prevented him from
writing it. The poem that Shelley wanted to write
"hung for a while above the Mediterranean, and then
drifted up toward the Tyrol," where Ibsen caught it
and wrote it down as *The Master Builder*. " 'It is not
a strange idea, or a new one,' " says Shelley, " 'that
the stuff of which masterpieces are made drifts about
the world, waiting to be clothed in words.' "[3] However, this Platonic truth to some degree depreciates
the words in which the masterpiece is couched. " 'The
words of a masterpiece are the least of its offerings.' "[4]

At the beginning of this act of *The Master
Builder*, Shelley, the poet of *Epipsychidion* and *Pro-
metheus Unbound*, after mentioning the machines
and constructions of this twentieth century, says:
" 'My poems must seem very strange in a world of
such things.' "[5]

But in the sphere of the real within actuality the
sentimental is absent, even in a poetical sense. The
language in this surrealistic realm is handled in ex-
actly the same way as in the realm of the actual,
without solemnity, as though both were on the same
level of existence. Indeed, in "Leviathan," the two
realms seem actually interchangeable: the realm of

the prince, who is sleeping in the sea and is awakened by the mermaid, seems to be the realm "beyond," and the legendary realm of the mermaid seems to be actuality. The prince does not see the mermaid as she believes herself to be, but, to her astonishment, as a phantom.

In the play "And the Sea Shall Give Up Its Dead" the trumpet of the last judgment day dies away "in the remotest pockets of space. . . . Several miles below the surface of the North Atlantic, the spirits of the drowned rise through the water like bubbles in a neglected wineglass."[6] Some of these drowned spirits—the Empress of Newfoundland, a stout little Jew who was a former theatrical manager, and a priest—rise up and talk to each other about their experiences. The Empress declares: " 'We still cling obstinately to our identity, as though there were something valuable in it.' "[7] They are terribly afraid of losing their identity when they reach the surface of the ocean:

The extensive business of Domesday is over in a twinkling and the souls divested of all identification have tumbled like shooting stars into the blaze of unicity. Soon nothing exists in space but the great unwinking eye meditating a new creation.[8]

If these plays have a religious meaning, they are nevertheless without any pathos. What was observable in the novels also applies here: there is an absence of sentimentality and solemnity, a relaxed ease despite their compact brevity, and, not least, a restrained humor. The donkey Hepzibah, who in the

play "Flight into Egypt" carries Our Lady and the
child, accompanied by the old man, into Egypt, stops
every few minutes because she is tired. She goes on
talking wisely, although Herod's soldiers are at her
heels and every delay is dangerous. This Hepzibah is
decidedly funny with her chatter about faith and
reason: " 'Well, well, it's a queer world where the
survival of the Lord is dependent on donkeys.' "9

In "Now the Servant's Name Was Malchus,"
Christ is placed in a somewhat cosmic office in
heaven. The angel Gabriel, a sort of orderly, conveys
messages and submits documents to him. At the out-
set of the play, Malchus is watching at the ordering
of the "cases" of the deceased. He is the servant whose
ear Peter cut off when Jesus was taken into captivity.
Malchus tells Christ that he now would like to
be deleted from the book telling about this event
(he says, incidentally, that it was the left ear, not the
right one) because he feels that people on earth regard him as ridiculous. But even Christ thinks he has
made himself ridiculous because his promises to human beings were so vast that he must be either divine
or ridiculous. " 'Malchus, will you stay and be ridiculous with me?' "10 Malchus consents only too gladly.

Quite the most amusing character is Satan in
"Hast Thou Considered My Servant Job?" which
parodies the writing style of the Bible. Just as Satan
once made a wager with God about Job, so Christ and
Satan make a wager about Judas, whom Satan gives
into the hands of Christ. In the end Christ suffers a
more complete defeat than Satan himself anticipated.

" 'Even Judas, even when my power was withdrawn from him, even Judas betrayed you.' "[11] And the master of Hell, who builds on the indomitable passions of greed, lust, and self-love, wants to assure Judas of Hell's highest honors. Judas appears with downcast eyes, and, when Christ bids him address Satan, he says to Satan: " 'Accursed be thou from eternity to eternity.' "[12] And then "these two [Christ and Judas] mount upward to their due place, and Satan remains to this day, uncomprehending, upon the pavement of Hell."[13]

The compact brevity of these plays, as well as the informality of treatment, permitted Wilder to move freely into a realm beyond actuality. Characteristically, he did not lapse into romantic subjectivism. Even the objects of his free-roving imagination are accurately, though not emotionally, portrayed. One recognizes in them Wilder's effort to achieve the at-homeness with how one sees, feels, and says things in English—as he felt Madame de Sévigné had done in French. His plays as well as his novels read smoothly and effortlessly.

5

The Woman
of Andros

In 1930, three years after *The Bridge of San Luis Rey*, Wilder published his next novel, *The Woman of Andros*. With this novel he goes back to the late Hellenic age. The material is derived from *Andria*, a comedy of the Latin playwright Terence, who in turn based his work upon two comedies of the Greek dramatist and poet Menander. Thus, once again, the American utilized elements of European tradition, as he did in *The Cabala*, but this time he reached far back into ancient pagan civilization.

The comedy of Terence (circa 190–160 B.C.) takes place in Athens where young Pamphilus, son of Simo, falls in love with the sister of the hetaera Chrysis—the woman of Andros—who was forced to take up this profession when she came to Athens. But because Pamphilus is supposed to marry the daughter of his neighbor Chremes, all kinds of complications arise that are happily resolved when it is discovered that Glycerium, the "sister" of Chrysis—who has meanwhile died—is a daughter of Chremes. Thus, Pamphilus is able to marry her.

Wilder uses the story, but changes almost everything except the names. To begin with, he removes the scene from Athens to the island of Brynos and to an insignificant port by the same name—in other words, to a small-town, bourgeois environment. The fathers, Simo and Chremes, are well-to-do merchants and leading citizens of the community, but both find the appearance of the hetaera Chrysis a threat to the ancient and honorable order of the island. They feel that with her symposia, in which she recites the classic tragedies and stimulates discussions, she is adding an unwanted foreign element to the modest cultural requirements of the community. Chremes takes Simo to task because he permits his son Pamphilus to visit the house of Chrysis, when for years it has been agreed that he was to marry Chremes's daughter. Simo, the more broadminded of the two men, would like to continue giving his son a certain amount of freedom.

Chrysis is thus an unwitting obstacle. It is she whom Wilder makes the focal point of the novel. She dies, and at her funeral it becomes apparent that Pamphilus loves Glycerium, Chrysis's sister, and that this girl is carrying his child. Simo finally reveals a sense of humanity by taking the pregnant girl into his house when she is about to be taken into slavery. But Glycerium dies when her child is born.

Terence's suspenseful but gay comedy has turned into a story weighted with human sorrow and suffering. Yet, in contrast to *The Bridge of San Luis Rey*, the burden of pessimism seems somewhat lightened by the entire atmosphere, by the restraint of the outward show of emotions, the tenderness of the young lovers, and the spirituality of the hetaera Chrysis.

The idea of inadequate family ties appears again in this novel. The relationship between Chrysis and her sister is contrasted with the bourgeois families of Simo and Chremes. Both women are defenseless against their fate, thrown back on their own resources.

The meaning of the story, however, is revealed

above all in the figure of Chrysis. In the comedy of
Terence she is a hetaera like any other of ancient
Greece. Here she has become a highly differentiated
figure of a woman who both intellectually and personally is far superior to her environment, even to
Simo, whose social position is all but unattainable to
her. She loves Pamphilus and experiences the agony
of a woman whose love is not returned. She helps
others by taking stray human beings into her household—all the while she herself stretches out her hands
toward emptiness.

Wilder seems to be concerned throughout his
works with the question How does one live? This is
especially so in *The Woman of Andros*. Chrysis, at
one of her banquets, tells the story of a hero who has
rendered Zeus a great service. After his death, he
begged Zeus to let him return to earth for one day.
Zeus, at first greatly troubled, succeeded in gaining
permission from the King of the Dead to let the hero
live over again the least eventful day of his earthly
life, but on condition that he live it as two persons:
the participant and the onlooker.

"Suddenly the hero saw that the living too are dead and
that we can only be said to be alive in those moments
when our hearts are conscious of our treasure; for our
hearts are not strong enough to love every moment."[1]

Not an hour had gone by before the hero begged Zeus
to release him from so terrible a dream.

Pamphilus, who was among the guests of the
symposium, now saw with new eyes "the secret life
of his parent's minds. It seemed suddenly as though

he saw behind the contentment and the daily talka-
tiveness into the life of their hearts—empty, resigned,
pathetic, and enduring."[2] And he sees that this will
soon be his own lot, that he will soon be a husband
and a father, the head of a household. He will grow
old:

Time would have flowed by him like a sigh, with no plan
made, no rules set, no strategy devised that would have
taught him how to save these others and himself from
the creeping gray, from the too-easily accepted frustration. "How does one live?" he asked the bright sky.
"What does one do first?"[3]

This question How does one live? is a question
often asked by Chrysis.

It was her reiterated theory of life that all human beings
—save a few mysterious exceptions who seem to be in
possession of some secret from the gods—merely endure
the slow misery of existence, hiding as best they could
their consternation that life had no wonderful surprises
after all and that its most difficult burden was the in-
communicability of love.[4]

At the center of the story stands the image of a
young priest of Apollo, an uncommonly simple figure, removed from all temporal human ties. The
young priest has taken the vow of celibacy; he
drinks no wine and lives on fruits and vegetables.
But he is somewhat of an athlete. He never entered
the competitive games, but he runs six miles every
day, and his vow, "when profoundly encompassed,
fills the mind with such power that it is forever cut
off from the unstable tentative sons of men."[5] This

priest, in a manner unexpressed, anticipates the
Saviour whose coming is indicated at the beginning
and at the end.

But Wilder seems also to imply that, while
struggling to realize a world beyond the present, one
cannot renounce this world. Chrysis, the moment she
begins to love Pamphilus (who, it was said by the
people of Brynos, has some priestlike qualities in
him), has an agonizing insight:

It was true, true beyond a doubt, tragically true, that the
world of love and virtue and wisdom was the true world
and her failure in it all the more overwhelming. But she
was not alone; he too saw the long and failing war as
she did, and she loved him. . . .[6]

And on her deathbed she confesses to Pamphilus:

". . . let me say now . . . ," her hands opened and closed
upon the clothes that covered her, ". . . I want to say
to someone . . . that I have known the worst that the
world can do to me, and that nevertheless I praise the
world and all living. All that is, is well."[7]

Later, when Pamphilus thinks of the dead Chrysis, he
remembers

her strange command to him that he praise all life, even
the dark . . . his depression, like a cloud, drifted away
from him and he was filled with a tremulous happiness.
He too praised the whole texture of life, for he saw how
strangely life's richest gift flowered from frustration and
cruelty and separation. . . . It seemed to him that the
whole world did not consist of rocks and trees and water
nor were human beings garments and flesh, but all
burned, like the hillside of olive trees, with the perpetual
flame of love. . . . But why then a love so defeated, as

though it were waiting for a void to come from the skies, declaring therein lay the secret of the world.[8]

And Pamphilus knew "that a sun would rise and before that sun the timidity and the hesitation would disappear. . . . He strode forward, his arms raised to the sky in joyous gratitude, and as he went he cried: 'I praise all living, the bright and the dark.' "[9]

But his exhilaration vanishes with the death of his beloved and his child. The others in his family now turn to him and try to read from his face

what news there was from the last resources of courage and hope, to live on, to live by. But in confusion and with flagging courage he repeated: "I praise all living, the bright and the dark."[10]

The novel is epic in character simply because it takes place in a narrow and definitely circumscribed milieu, the island of Brynos. With deliberate yet spare realism the daily life of the island is described: the market, the palaestra, the harbor, the insignificant—and yet so significant—lives of human beings. The landscape seems to encompass more than an occasional vista. Pamphilus wanders to the highest point of the island: "It was early spring. A strong wind had blown every cloud from the sky and the sea lay covered with flying, white-tipped waves."[11] The steep land, the occasional view of the sea at dusk, the shadowy profile of Andros on the horizon, the ships in the harbor, the comfortable busyness of the inhabitants, the heat of the day and the cool breeze at night—all give the work, slight as it is, an epic

breadth and distinction, a definitiveness that things
will always remain the same. Yet this vision is ever
so slightly disturbed by the hint of an approaching,
unknown change, by the possibility that one day
things may be different. That is why the novel is introduced by a kind of description of the ancient world
that is not usually encountered: the earth sighing as
it turned in its course, the shadow of night creeping
along the Mediterranean from an Asia left in darkness.

In this description, which finally brings into
focus "the happiest and least famous" of the islands,
Brynos, there appears, after Egypt and Greece, after
Sicily around which a storm is playing, "the land that
was soon to be called Holy," and that was preparing
"in the dark its wonderful burden."[12] That land is
again referred to in the epilogue, and thus the passage
of time is suggested: "And in the East the stars shone
tranquilly down upon the land that was soon to be
called Holy and that even then was preparing its
precious burden."[13] In the simplest words, the world's
turning point, the world's hour is foretold.

The actual suspense of the novel lies in this contrast between local limitation and world scope. It is
a dramatic suspense. This uniting of the epic and the
dramatic is characteristic of *The Woman of Andros*.
The tense conversations begin with the argument between Chremes and Simo in the wineshop. Chremes
urges his friend to make Pamphilus marry his daughter Philumena, but Simo sullenly evades the issue.

The conversation, which is not developed without humor, gives a complete exposition, informing the reader not only about the family circumstances of the two fathers and the character of Pamphilus, but also about Chrysis, the woman of Andros, and her situation. The later conversations, too, are tense discussions, dialogues in the true sense of the word: the nocturnal conversation between Simo and Chrysis at the harbor; the conversation between Pamphilus and Glycerium at their first meeting; the scene in which Glycerium confesses to Chrysis her relationship with Pamphilus and her condition. Indeed, even the one-sided conversation of Simo with Pamphilus in the palaestra is of the same character as the earlier conversations—Simo tries to arrange in his mind his objections to his son's union with Glycerium, the hetaera's sister, finally realizing that Pamphilus has gone to sleep and that he is carrying on the dialogue with himself.

In this work Wilder reached a high point in his artistic development. The composition, in the fusion of the epic and the dramatic, is almost faultless. *The Bridge of San Luis Rey*, in its subject matter alone, may have had a suspense that, in the story of *The Woman of Andros*, seems to be present only in two points: the prologue and the epilogue. But this is only apparently so; the actual tension in *The Woman of Andros* lies in the almost greater meaninglessness of the individual lives it portrays. In the story of the five victims of the catastrophe the very scene of the action suggests hidden explosive forces within that remote, volcanically undermined country of the Inca civilization. In the present novel, the gentler and more delicate tension, softened by the idyllic setting, leads to a warmth that Wilder could scarcely have surpassed.

6

One-Act
Plays

The one-act plays in the collection entitled *The Long Christmas Dinner*, which appeared in 1931, move a little more in a world of actuality. In the title play and in "Pullman Car Hiawatha," however, the dimensions of time and distance are ignored. This is also true to a certain extent of the play "The Happy Journey to Trenton and Camden," in which an auto ride of four or five hours takes place in twenty minutes. "Queens of France" and "Love and How to Cure It" are more conventional in these respects.

The most remarkable of these plays is "The Long Christmas Dinner," in which a dinner continues uninterruptedly from 1840 to 1930, through the various generations. It is always Christmas Day, but the family members change, exiting through a portal at the right when they die. The stage directions still pay some heed to the audience's need for actuality:

At the extreme left, by the proscenium pillar, is a strange portal trimmed with garlands of fruits and flowers. Directly opposite is another edged and hung with black velvet. The portals denote birth and death. . . . The actors are dressed in inconspicuous clothes and must indicate their gradual increase in years through their acting. Most of them carry wigs of white hair which they adjust upon their heads at the indicated moment, simply and without comment. . . . Throughout the play the characters continue eating imaginary food with imaginary knives and forks. There is no curtain. . . .[1]

The conversation of the characters is on an ordinary level; they talk about the weather, about the family and its connections, about the ever-receding past. Throughout generations the same observations are made: " 'Every least twig is wrapped around with ice. You almost never see that.' "[2] Children are born, marry, and die. Finally, Aunt Ermengarde alone is left in the house that was brand-new at the play's opening. "She grows from very old to immensely old. She sighs. The book falls down. She finds a cane beside her, and soon totters into the dark portal, murmuring: 'Dear little Roderick and little Lucia.' "[3]

"The Happy Journey to Trenton and Camden" is almost as remarkable, since Wilder, in anticipation of *Our Town*, uses practically no scenery. This one-act play is set in almost the same small-town, middle-class environment as *Our Town*. A family consisting of parents and three children go on a three-day trip to visit a married daughter living in another city. The ride in an automobile—represented by a few chairs and steered by gestures—lasts all afternoon, but occupies only about twenty minutes in the play. Here the Stage Manager himself enters the action, reading a part occasionally and addressing comments, explanations, and suggestions to the audience.

In the one-act play "Pullman Car Hiawatha," the Stage Manager, after some introductory explanations, calls the actors onstage, and they take their places. The stage is entirely free of properties and scenery. The Pullman is en route from New York to Chicago on a night in December. The Stage Manager claps his hands, and the town of Grover's Corners enters and speaks his few lines. A field enters, a tramp, the town of Parkersburg. The weather enters, and the hours—representing Plato, Epictetus, and Augustine, from whose writings they recite—pass slowly across the back. The planets appear and sing. "Stage Manager: 'Louder, Saturn.—Venus, higher. Good. Now Jupiter. . . . Now the earth.' "[4] Finally, they all sing together, and the Stage Manager conducts, "as the director of an orchestra would." One of the passengers dies. The Archangels Gabriel and Michael, two young men in serge suits, enter to get the dead woman.

Thus the lively action continues in this sleeping car represented by no scenery except a few chalk marks and a few chairs. It is a strange but utterly natural mixture of quite banal realism and dreamlike fantasy that nevertheless seems "real."

7

Heaven's My Destination

In answer to the criticism of literary observers that he was apparently inclined to avoid the problems of present-day America, Wilder published the novel *Heaven's My Destination* (1935). With it he proved that he did not hesitate to set a novel in the twentieth century, even to set it in the immediate present, the period of the Great Depression. He showed himself quite capable of portraying an American similar to those who exist in the realistic literature of the United States. Even the numerous secondary figures of the story, in their conversations and views about life, behave like average Americans.

The story extends from the twenty-third to the twenty-fourth birthday of its hero, George Brush. He is a very efficient salesman for a textbook publisher; so efficient in fact that, notwithstanding the Depression, he is given a raise. This young man, however, has taken Gandhi as his example and wants to live according to the principles of voluntary poverty and (in spite of an unusually strong physique) nonviolence, the *ahimsa* of his model. Brush endeavors to translate religious ideas directly into life, to be a missionary as it were. Opposed to smoking and drinking, he seeks to persuade others to forgo these vices. He scrawls biblical texts and edifying admonitions on hotel blotters. He withdraws his money from a bank, but refuses the interest for religious reasons, and makes a speech to the president, who has him arrested. When in Kansas City, he usually spends the night in a shabby boardinghouse, where he sings quartets with a few buddies. But they finally play a trick on their innocent companion: they get him drunk, and on the pretext of inviting him to the home of an elegant lady who has many pretty daughters, they take him to a brothel. He is enchanted with so much beauty and takes the girls to the movies. But later the men enlighten him, and in a paroxysm of hatred, they beat him up so badly that he is taken to the hospital.

"God didn't give you any brains," Louie, one of the men, says to him. And the apostle of nonviolence confesses: "That's the third time that people have suddenly hated me."[1] Louie tries to encourage him to be like other, "sensible" people, but at that Brush bursts out: "If you must know, I'm not crazy. It's the world that's crazy. Everybody's crazy except me; that's what's the matter. The whole world's nuts."[2]

Brush's innocence involves him in situations for which he would certainly have to pay dearly if this very innocence did not, time and again, also extricate him from predicaments. His idea of *ahimsa* even lands him in prison because he is quite unjustly suspected of a holdup in a small shop.

The novel consists of a series of such adventures, partly depressing, partly amusing, in which George Brush constantly provokes anger and makes himself ridiculous. It could almost be considered a picaresque novel (in keeping with the chapter headings, which briefly summarize the contents) were it not for the ambivalent feelings that the hero arouses. This "saint" is by no means unlikable. Yet, in the long run, his extreme naïveté becomes repugnant or, at any rate, disagreeable. The child's doggerel verse from which the title is derived is actually meant to warn the reader not to take the hero too seriously.

Brush's lack of intelligence, or insight, causes him to misunderstand what religion is all about: he fights sin by trying only to remove its symptoms. He is not able to grasp the reality of his fellowmen; the moral rules of life that he urges on them are only abstractions. He does not realize that that is the reason he offends. Because he cannot arrive at any self-knowledge, his life is a failure. Even his marriage, with which he tries to rectify a previous mistake and to found a genuine American home filled with peace and purity and uprightness—even this proves a failure. Occasionally he does actually help in desperate cases: he prevents a financially ruined man from committing suicide; he adopts the little daughter of his friend Herb, and the child loves him. But essentially he fails because he cannot establish contact with human beings.

Finally, out of complete dejection, Brush gives himself up to a worldly life for a short time: he buys a pipe and tobacco; he laughs and talks a lot, and tries to enjoy himself: "One day he arose to discover, quite simply, that he had lost his faith. . . . At first his only emotion was astonishment. He looked about him; he had mislaid something that would turn up presently. But it did not turn up. . . ."[3] A cynical exhilaration takes hold of him.

Shortly after this experience he falls ill. For weeks he lies apathetically in the hospital; so seriously

ill that a clergyman calls on him. The man's unctuous
words awaken his slumbering energies. He thinks he
has at last found proof that there is no God because
such foolish people are allowed to be ministers. Brush
begins shouting at the horrified minister: "I've secretly thought that for a long time, and now I'm glad
to be able to say it. All ministers are stupid—do you
hear me?—*all*. . . . I mean: all except one."[4]

That one is Father Pasziewski who suffers from
gallstones—but even more from his failure to influence his flock. He is referred to on three occasions,
but does not actually appear in the novel. He is a
sort of parallel figure to George Brush insofar as
his spiritual efforts reap nothing but failure, just as
the importunate evangelist on the train to Dallas
("Young man, have you ever thought seriously about
the facts of life and death?"[5]) is somewhat of a parallel figure, though at the same time a contrast to the
much more ingenuous, honest, and pure George
Brush. Father Pasziewski knows Brush only from
hearsay; but he prays for him, and, when Father
Pasziewski dies that same year, he leaves him a sil-
ver-plated spoon. From that day on, Brush begins to
get well.

Perhaps the mysterious figure of Father Pasziewski subtly suggests that Brush is not altogether
mistaken in thinking that everybody in the world is
wrong except himself. Wilder has an inclination toward such mystification, and it would also be in keeping with his sense of humor.

Brush recovers: he again becomes the heaven-

sent "fool in Christ." Again he is confined in jail for
a few hours. "The charge was later found to have
been based on a misunderstanding. He was released
and continued on his journey."[6] The novel ends in a
pessimism that now seems hopeless—unless the existence of the fool in Christ proves to be indispensable
to human society, which, alongside or beyond or in
the midst of its worldly needs, also has its spiritual
needs.

In comparison with the earlier works, this novel
seems rather formless, almost improvised. There is,
however, a certain rhythm: the hero's twofold break-
down—the first time in Kansas City after the episode
in the brothel, the second time when he falls ill after
attempting to lead a worldly life—divides the book
into three parts. But having demonstrated the con-
flicts of the world on the basis of contemporary figures, Wilder put them aside and has not yet returned
to them. George Brush was not the man to become
Wilder's Gulliver or Robinson Crusoe.

8

Three Plays

In his Preface to *Three Plays* (1957) Wilder tells why, though consciously traditional in his narrative technique, he adopted such a revolutionary course as a dramatist. Toward the end of the 1920s he began to find the traditional theater inadequate, even at its best. He was still able to admire the work of a great actor or director or designer, and he was convinced that the theater

was the greatest of all the arts [but that it was] fulfilling only a small part of its potentialities. . . . I was like a schoolmaster grading a paper; to each of these offerings I gave an A+, but the condition of mind of one grading a paper is not that of one being overwhelmed by an artistic creation. The response we make when we "believe" a work of the imagination is that of saying: "This is the way things are, I have always known it without being fully aware that I knew it. Now in the presence of this play or novel (or picture or piece of music) I know that I know it." It is this form of knowledge which Plato called "recollection." We have all murdered in thought; and been murdered. We have all seen the ridiculous in estimable persons and in ourselves.[1]

The theater, he continues, is best adapted to awaken this "recollection" within us. However, he denied it the belief he was ready to bring to the works of a James Joyce, a Proust, or a Thomas Mann. He realized that the theater, as it presented itself to the audience, with all its picturesque adjuncts simulating reality and nature, aimed for a "soothing" effect.

The tragic had no heat; the comic had no bite; the social criticism failed to indict us with responsibility. I began to search for the point where the theater had run off the track, where it had chosen—and been permitted—to become a minor art and an inconsequential diversion.[2]

This point Wilder found in the rise of the middle class in the nineteenth century. The middle class, which became absolutely dominant in the United States, in Scandinavia, and in Germany, had forgotten that it was once a class despised by the aristocracy and the peasantry. It had been obliged to fight for acceptance by making and accumulating money in order to justify itself in the eyes of the aristocracy. The aristocracy, in an attempt to further its interests and its alleged moral and cultural superiority, now enjoyed the atmosphere and the elegance of the arts, but not their substance. The newly rich middle class, however, had a degenerating effect on the theater because it expected from the theater the same thing it expected from life. It wanted its theater soothing. It wanted to be able to close its eyes to the injustices of the world, the passions, the problems that were everywhere but that no one was permitted to discuss—in short, it wanted to shut out everything that might deprive it of its sense of security. Thus the theater, with its circumscribed stage and its illusionistic equipment, "smothered" even Shakespeare and increasingly severed drama from life. In consequence, it was no longer taken seriously.

Wilder points out why the box-set stage had such a stifling effect. Every action, he says, represents something completely and irrevocably individual, a uniqueness, even though it has happened many millions of times. The sentence "I love you" has been spoken countless times, but never twice in the same way. Yet we are aware that these countless moments have something in common.

The theatre is admirably fitted to tell both truths. It has one foot planted firmly in the particular, since each actor before us (even when he wears a mask!) is indubitably a living, breathing "one"; yet it tends and strains to exhibit a general truth. . . . It is through the theatre's power to raise the exhibited individual action into the realm of idea and type and universal that it is able to evoke our belief.[3]

It was this power that the nineteenth-century audience did not dare confront. They tamed it by squeezing it into a showcase, by cluttering the stage with objects, and shifting into the past the action that was supposed to take place "now." Thus, all the figures were already dead before the action began. The childish attempt to be real led to a disbelief in what was portrayed; for in giving the space of the stage reality one also fixes the time. In trying to be real the theater was saying only one truth, the particular truth that did not basically concern the audience.

In the Chinese theater an actor rides a stick to show riding a horse, and in the Japanese noh play the actor walks around the stage to portray a lengthy journey. Wilder, in plays such as those in *The Long Christmas Dinner* or in *Our Town*, uses similar devices to portray not verisimilitude but reality.

Our Town, a full-length play in three acts, appeared in 1938. It begins with the following stage directions:

No curtain. No scenery.
The audience, arriving, sees an empty stage in half-light.
Presently the Stage Manager, hat on and pipe in mouth,
enters and begins placing a table and several chairs down
stage left, and a table and chairs down stage right.
As the house lights go down he has finished setting the
stage and leaning against the right proscenium pillar
watches the late arrivals in the audience.
When the auditorium is in complete darkness he speaks.[4]

One senses a good deal of indefinable irony in the role of the Stage Manager. He begins very matter-of-factly: " 'This play is called "Our Town." It was written by Thornton Wilder; produced and directed by————. , . . In it you will see————.' " He introduces the actors, gives the name of the town, and tells where it is located. He gives the date: May 7, 1901, just before dawn. He makes a rather long speech describing the town; he tells something about the characters who first appear, even permitting himself to anticipate the future: Doc Gibbs, who appears on the stage this May 7, 1901, died in 1930. The new hospital was named after him. Mrs. Gibbs died first—a long time ago. Meanwhile, "Mrs. Gibbs has entered the kitchen, gone through the motions of putting wood into a stove, lighting it, and preparing breakfast."[5]

The Stage Manager not only reports about the town of Grover's Corners, he actually directs the play, cuts off dialogues (" 'Thank you, Mrs. Webb. Thank

you, Emily.' "), introduces new speeches, announces
the hours, and keeps the audience informed about
what is happening. Now and then he plays some part
himself, such as the owner of the drugstore where
Emily and George have their decisive conversation
and the minister who marries them. He also brings
the play to a close: " 'Most everybody's asleep in
Grover's Corners. There are a few lights on. . . .
There are the stars—doing their old, old crisscross
journeys in the sky.' "[6] He winds his watch, announces that it is an hour before midnight, and wishes
the audience good night.

Wilder states in his Preface to *Three Plays* that
he wrote *Our Town* in an effort to "find a value above
all price for the smallest events of our daily life."[7]
He even tries to underline the minutiae that make up
the lives of the two small-town families, the Gibbses
and Webbs and their children, by contrasting them
with the universality of the millions and millions of
times that similar things have occurred. This idea of
the contrast between the minute and the universal—
which is at the same time a harmony—is especially
apparent when, at the end of the first act, Rebecca
Gibbs tells her brother George about the letter that a
friend of hers received from a minister. On the en-
velope, besides the usual details of the address, was
written: "the United States of America; Continent of
North America; Western Hemisphere; the Earth; the
Solar System; the Universe; the Mind of God."[8]

Characters and action acquire a meaning in relation to the universal, the "mind of God." They are

not individualized by stage properties that could destroy that relationship. This becomes most evident at the end of the third act in the cemetery scene. Emily, who has recently died, appears while her burial is taking place in the background. The dead, among them Emily's mother-in-law, watch the action calmly. Emily has not yet become accustomed to her new position; she wants to go back and live over again an actual day of her life. She chooses her twelfth birthday, February 11, 1899. The dead warn her that she will not only live the day over again but will watch herself living it. Soon she discovers that she cannot bear it. " 'It goes so fast,' " she complains. " 'Oh, earth, you're too wonderful for anybody to realize you.' "[9] And in tears she asks the Stage Manager: " 'Do any human beings ever realize life while they live it?—every, every minute?' "[10] The Stage Manager replies: " 'No. . . . The saints and poets, maybe—they do some.' "[11] And Emily is quite willing to go back to the realm of the dead.

It is the Stage Manager who gives the play its unique, almost improvised character and yet makes it appear as something "enduring." It is he who holds the threads in his hand, who knows everything and yet gives the characters the freedom to choose what they wish to do. He does not state the meaning—the meaning is implied in the interplay of characters. Here, too, there are no sentimental overtones. There is no intrusion of "actuality" until the third act. But again the meaning of life remains an open question; the Stage Manager's reply that the saints and poets may perhaps realize life to a certain extent is too vague to be more than a suggestion. Nevertheless, one feels a slight change here. The impression that the problem of life's meaning remains unanswered does not exclude a deeper impression that there is a meaning.

Whereas Wilder's novels (with the exception of *Heaven's My Destination*) owed so much to the spirit of Greece and Rome, with a Christian background, that superficially one might conclude they were written by a European, this is not true of the plays. These could have been written only by an American. In the drama, Wilder seems to have found his own form to express the ideas that basically mattered to him.

The Skin of Our Teeth, which appeared in 1942, seems to confirm this. The play has been criticized for being an historico-philosophical book drama containing a bloodless theory of history. From the formal point of view, *The Skin of Our Teeth* represents something positively revolutionary. But with it, Wilder—who raises such basic questions as: What shall we eat? What shall we drink?—was able to grasp the reality of the present. It became a hit throughout a world in which the very existence of man is at stake, and later it made an especially deep impression on the defeated of World War II, for whom the announcement that there is a recipe for grass soup that does not give one diarrhea was met with a good deal of understanding.

In *The Skin of Our Teeth* the stage manager does

not direct the play nor have a central role in it, as he does in *Our Town*. He merely fills in when Miss Somerset, the stage character playing Sabina, misses her cue or becomes contrary to her role. He does not hold the threads of the whole performance in his hands.

The announcer, who introduces and explains the situation at the beginning of the first and second acts, has the function of replacing the sets of the traditional play; the various scenes are supplied with the most essential properties. The setting is not quite as abstract as in *Our Town*: the house in which the Antrobus family lives at least has walls, though now and then they lean over or fly up into the loft. The play, however, might approximate a conventional stage setting were it not for the constant shifting of reality whose puzzling complexity—though it seems entirely "natural"—belies any such approximation. In fact, the levels of reality are shifted about to such an extent that it does not seem very important to distinguish between them. This, in addition to the fact that the cast of characters is almost twice as large, makes a strict absence of scenery not as necessary as in *Our Town*.

Again the fate of a family is portrayed. (It is interesting to note that Wilder the dramatist places the family at the center of the action—a position that Wilder the novelist avoids.) This is the story of Mr. and Mrs. Antrobus and their two children, Gladys and Henry. The family name and the content of the play suggest that this is basically a story of man (*anthropos*) or of Adam and Eve and their son Cain, who killed his brother.

There are two time levels in the play: the present of the audience and a constantly shifting time level. The Antrobus family lives in Excelsior, New Jersey, takes part in a convention in Atlantic City, and, in the third act, is back in its home in Excelsior. But in the first act the Ice Age threatens, in the second the Flood occurs, and in the third a modern world war has just ended.

The first act takes place in an average suburban home whose owner, Mr. Antrobus, returns from his office in New York. A small dinosaur and a baby mammoth move about the house, having sought shelter indoors from a glacial movement that, in the middle of August, has brought the temperature down far below freezing. A band of refugees appears: Homer, Moses, three of the nine Muses. Mr. Antrobus has invented the wheel and the alphabet, which he is trying to perfect—he has just separated em from en. His son, Henry, some time ago killed his older brother and bears the mark of Cain on his forehead. The maid, Sabina, moves in and out among the family, exercising her right to give two weeks' notice. Miss Somerset, the actress playing the role of Sabina, now and then misses her cue or refuses to continue because she does not "understand" the play.

The second act is more in the sphere of actuality. But here, too, at the convention of Mammals, subdivision Humans, there are "irregularities." Sabina, now a beauty queen, charming hostess of a bingo parlor, and seductress of Mr. Antrobus, again suddenly steps out of her role. She refuses to continue in the scene with Mr. Antrobus because she has a female friend in the audience, in front of whom she does not wish to speak certain lines: " 'I don't suppose it occurred to the author that some other women might have gone through the experience of losing their husbands like this. Wild horses . . .' "[12] The stage manager, Mr. Fitzpatrick, has a hard time with the sensitive actress, who manages to have her own way. Mr. Antrobus himself approves of skipping the scene.

Meanwhile, the third of several black discs indicating hurricane warnings has already appeared on the weather signal. A storm soon breaks loose, but the Antrobus family escapes in a boat. Henry-Cain is also saved, along with Sabina: " 'Mrs. Antrobus—take me. Don't you remember me? I'll work.' "[13] Only the "conveners," who have amused themselves in senseless pleasures, remain behind: " 'You've failed. You've lost.' "[14]

In the third act the scene is back in the Antrobuses' house following the most recent world war. Sabina is again the maid, dressed as a Napoleonic camp follower, and it is she who starts the action and keeps it moving.

At the beginning of this act the stage manager finds himself obliged to introduce laymen to play the roles of several actors who have been taken ill. These roles are the hours that Wilder, as in "Pullman Car

Hiawatha," assigned to a number of philosophers and to the Bible. At this point the laymen briefly rehearse their scene in anticipation of the end, and Sabina then starts the act again from the beginning.

Of all the trials that he must go through, the actual difficulty for Antrobus-Adam—and this is the point at which Wilder's play becomes relevant to the present—is the existence of his son Henry-Cain. He who as a boy slew his brother is now the "representative of strong, irreconcilable evil"; in other words, of individualism carried to extremes. When his father threatens him with a gun, Henry says: " 'I haven't got anybody over me; and I never will have. I'm alone, and that's all I want to be: alone.' "[15] His father replies:

"The sight of you dries up all my plans and hopes. I wish I were back at war still, because it's easier to fight you than to live with you. War's a pleasure—do you hear me?—War's a pleasure compared to what faces us now: trying to build up a peace time with you in the middle of it."[16]

Henry retorts that he is leaving: " 'I'm going a long way from here and make my own world that's fit for a man to live in. Where a man can be free, and have a chance, and do what he wants to do in his own way.' "[17] When Henry says that he wants to build "a world of free men," Antrobus throws down the gun and turns to Henry with hope that he may be able to work with his son. But at once the son destroys this hope: " 'Oh, no. I'll make a world, and I'll show you.' "[18]

Then Antrobus says something decisive:

"How can you make a world for people to live in, unless you first put order in yourself? . . . I shall continue fighting you until my last breath as long as you mix up your idea of liberty with your idea of hogging everything for yourself. I shall have no pity on you. I shall pursue you to the far corners of the earth. You and I want the same thing; but until you think of it as something that everyone has a right to, you are my deadly enemy and I will destroy you."[19]

Again the play's reality is interrupted, this time by the actor playing Henry-Cain. The scene shifts to the private life of the characters, making possible a certain solution to the conflict. Sabina—or rather Miss Somerset—throws herself between the opponents and separates them. The actor playing Henry, who has nothing personally against the actor playing Antrobus—who has, in fact, a high regard for him— claims he was incited to violence by the role he was playing. He confesses to a childhood trauma suffered when he was still under his parents' tyranny:

"It's like I had some big emptiness inside me—the emptiness of being hated and blocked at every turn. And the emptiness fills up with the one thought that you have to strike and fight and kill. Listen, it's as though you have to kill somebody else so as not to end up killing yourself."[20]

Sabina (Miss Somerset), with banal yet sound common sense, tries to tell him that this is not true, that he has imagined it all. Then the actor playing Antrobus speaks the redeeming lines of the scene:

"I have something to say, too. It's not wholly his fault
that he wants to strangle me in this scene. It's my fault,
too. He wouldn't feel that way unless there were something in me that reminded him of all that. He talks
about an emptiness. Well, there's an emptiness in me,
too. Yes—work, work, work—that's all I do. I've ceased
to *live*."[21]

It is the stage character who loses his temper,
and at first this seems to belong to the Henry-Cain
role: it would be consistent with this role if the son
strangled the father. When Miss Somerset intervenes
she could be addressing both Henry and the actor.
We have at this point the reality of the Henry-Cain
figure, the reality of the actor playing Henry, and
the reality of the actor playing the actor. Sabina and
Mr. and Mrs. Antrobus experience the same fluctua-
tions of reality in this scene, which is perhaps the
core of the play. Compared to such intricacy, the puz-
zle at the beginning of the third act, when the stage
manager interrupts Sabina, seems comparatively simple.

Mr. Antrobus, now in character again, goes on,
saying that he has lost the desire to begin again and
that he feels but one thing: relief that the war is over.
During the war, in all the dirt and blood, there were
always moments when he saw the things that could
be done when it was over. And then comes the frighteningly truthful statement to the effect that in war
one thinks about a better life, but in peacetime he
thinks about a more comfortable one.

Antrobus finds the way out of this impasse in
the memory of three things that have always given

him courage to believe in a new beginning: " 'The voice of the people in their confusion and their need. And the thought of you [his wife] and the children and this house.' "[22] The third is the thought of his books; that is, of the legacy of ideas, the voices of those who lead. " 'All I ask is the chance to build new worlds. And God has always given us that. . . . We've learned. We're learning.' "[23]

The play ends with aphorisms spoken by each of the hours: they include the words of Spinoza, about the vanity of the common occurrences of everyday life; of Plato, about the ruler who, before he rules, first establishes order in himself; of Aristotle, about the good estate of the mind, which is always present in God but only occasionally in mortals—wonderful in us but more wonderful by far in Him. The final hour, supporting the whole, recites the text of the biblical story of the creation: "In the beginning God created the heavens and the earth. . . ."

It is Sabina who is given the last lines of the play. She stands at the window, as at the beginning.

"Oh, oh, oh. Six o'clock and the master not home yet. . . ." She comes down to the footlights. "This is where you came in. We have to go on for ages and ages yet. You go home. The end of this play isn't written yet. Mr. and Mrs. Antrobus! Their heads are full of plans and they're as confident as the first day they began—and they told me to tell you: good night."[24]

The third play in the volume *Three Plays* is *The Matchmaker*, a slightly modified version of *The Merchant of Yonkers* (1938). The original comedy, or farce as Wilder calls it, was written between *Our Town* and *The Skin of Our Teeth* but has less creative substance than the two "abstract" dramas. Here Wilder used conventional scenery and properties. "One way to shake off the nonsense of the nineteenth-century staging," he wrote in the Preface, "is to make fun of it."[25]

The material is derived from the well-known farce *Einen Jux will er sich machen* (1842), by the Viennese playwright Johann Nestroy. Nestroy had in turn based his farce on John Oxenford's English original *A Day Well Spent* (1835). Wilder took over the action and characters of Nestroy's play and transferred them to New York City and the suburb Yonkers. The new character that he introduced, that of the matchmaker Dolly Levi, became the principal role in *The Matchmaker*. This slightly modified version was subsequently adapted into the popular musical "Hello, Dolly!"

The Viennese playwright took as his theme the wish of the shopkeeper, Weinberl, to be "a regular guy," to live grandly, like his employer. Wilder treats this in a more general way: the clerk Cornelius Hackl and the apprentice Barnaby Tucker take advantage of their boss's absence to go on a secret trip into New York City. But almost all the characters of the play cherish a secret desire to be able to live a freer life— even Mrs. Levi. It is she who finally traps Mr. Vandergelder, the wealthy merchant of Yonkers, into marrying her, almost against his wish and in defiance of all the subterfuges of the comedy.

At the end, Mrs. Levi takes the apprentice, Barnaby, aside and points to the audience, whereupon the boy stammers out the moral of the play:

"Oh, I think it's about . . . I think it's about adventure. The test of an adventure is that when you're in the middle of it, you say to yourself, 'Oh, now I've got myself into an awful mess; I wish I were sitting quietly at home.' And the sign that something's wrong with you is when you sit quietly at home wishing you were out having lots of adventure. . . . we all hope that in your lives you have just the right amount of—adventure!"[26]

The monologue of Dolly Levi in the last act is more substantial. In an aside to the audience she says that the mistakes we make by lavishly giving of ourselves do us less harm than the years we spend retiring into ourselves. The admonition to take people as they are, not to be afraid of making mistakes, goes beyond the farcical, no matter how lightly it is handled.

9

The Ides of March

In recent decades the figure of Caesar has engaged, with varying success, the imagination of a number of writers. (The warning of Hölderlin, the nineteenth-century German poet, not to make Napoleon the object of fiction could also be applied to the man whose name has become synonymous with supreme power on earth.) The age of the Roman revolution, the transition from the Republic to the Imperium, this age with its social unrest, its civil wars, it changing systems of sovereignty, its events of worldwide proportions, was too similar to our own, however, not to become a symbol of what can move human beings in public life.

Perhaps it was Wilder's desire to keep his subject near the "boundary of the unknown" or because he felt that the possibilities of a moral-ethical world could be discussed with more passion in an "old-world" context that he wrote *The Ides of March* (1948), the "novel" about Caesar.

The Ides of March, despite its brevity, is in its internal dimensions perhaps one of the most exhaustive and significant descriptions of that age, which, because of the inequalities of source material, permits only a "suppositional reconstruction," as Wilder writes in his prefatory note. Wilder properly calls the reader's attention to the form in which the voluminous material is supplied. The entire "novel" consists of documents, letters, reports, and, above all, the journal-letters of Caesar to Lucius Mamilius Turrinus. "All the documents," we read in the brief prefatory note, ". . . are from the author's imagination with the exception of the poems of Catullus and the closing entry, which is from Suetonius's *Lives of the Caesars*."[1] Two things are astonishing: the "genuineness" of these documents, letters, diaries, regulations, and descriptions, and the unidealized figure of Caesar himself. With *The Ides of March* Wilder, having already developed a revolutionary style in playwriting, became experimental with the novel form also. If the word "novel" is defined as something narrated, *The Ides of March* is not a novel: the narrative passages— Cleopatra's account of the garden party or Assinius Pollio's description of Clodia's dinner, recounted many years later from memory—are so isolated that they scarcely change the character of the whole. Helmut Papajewski has suggested that a more appropriate term might be "pseudo-factual report in novel form."[2]

The Ides of March is divided into four parts or "books," based on the latter months of Caesar's life. Book One consists of material supposedly written in September 45 B.C.; Book Two, the second half of August, the whole of September, and most of October of the same year; Book Three, the period from early August to approximately mid-December 45 B.C.; and Book Four, the seven and one-half months from early August 45 B.C. to the day in March 44 B.C. when Caesar was murdered.

As Wilder points out, the book is not an historical reconstruction but rather a "fantasia on certain events and persons of the last days of the Roman republic."[3] The author shifts a number of events and

persons into a period in which they do not belong:
the poet Catullus died long before this time, as did
Clodius; Cato the Younger committed suicide in 46
B.C., after the battle of Thapsus; and in the year
45 B.C., Caesar was no longer married to Pompeia
but to Calpurnia. The festival of the mysteries of the
Good Goddess, in which Clodius plays such a scan-
dalous part, took place some fifteen years earlier.

Another free invention is the figure of Turrinus,
the recipient of the journal-letters and the dictator's
confidential communications. It is possible that this
figure conceals the second of the two friends of Wilder
to whom the book is dedicated: Edward Sheldon,
"who though immobile and blind for over twenty
years was the dispenser of wisdom, courage, and
gaiety to a large number of people."[4] None of the
four parts contains any material written by Turrinus
himself: mutilated and blinded by the Belgians in the
Gallic Wars, he lives in retirement on the island of
Capri, and only Caesar, the actress Cytheris, and,
later, an aunt of Caesar are permitted to visit him
occasionally.

The characters seem altogether real, neither god-
like nor legendary. They are the exponents of a
worldly, very skeptical age marked by violence, civil
wars, moral instability, and cynical nihilism. Caesar,
the absolute monarch, plays the part of the reformer,
a role that ultimately destroys him. Basically, this
"novel" represents the struggle between the almost
solitary ruler and his own age, or rather the human

figures that personify that revolutionary age. The suspense, the excitement of the account, lies in the fact that even Caesar, with all his autonomous superiority and independence, is to a certain extent the product of his times.

In Caesar are exhibited all the imperfections of decaying Roman society. His relations with women, for example, are no different from those of his contemporaries; indeed, he is perhaps more of a libertine. He has secret police that make available to him numerous documents and letters not meant for his eyes. He is master over life and death to an extent that would have proved catastrophic in the hands of a weaker and less clear-minded ruler. He is the enlightened despot, who reorganizes the legal system, abolishes torture, regulates the course of the Tiber. Only indirectly does it become clear that Rome, at the beginning of Caesar's dictatorship, was one of the most corrupt states in history.

Two figures—Lady Clodia and her brother, Clodius Pulcher—represent the chaotic disorder that the dictator seeks to combat. Clodius writes nothing himself, but we learn enough about him to know that he is a Henry Antrobus who has sunk into complete moral depravity, into meaninglessness. The dictator scarcely deems him worthy of mentioning. The figure of the self-destructive Clodia is perhaps the most important as a foil to Caesar. Clodia and Caesar may be regarded as the protagonists of order and disorder, both tragic because they perish.

If Caesar scarcely mentions Clodius, he dwells
all the more in his journal-letters to Turrinus on
Clodia, whom he once admired as a gifted young girl.
But now he makes no effort to find excuses for her.
He speaks of her kind with no trace of compassion,
almost with contempt:

I am no longer immediately filled with compassion
when I encounter one of those innumerable persons who
trail behind them a shipwrecked life. Least of all do I
try to find excuses for them when I see that they have
found them for themselves, when I see them sitting on
the throne of their own minds, excused, acquitted, and
hurling indictments against the mysterious Destiny
which has wronged them and exhibiting themselves as
pure victim.[5]

He is concerned about building a political state in
which people need not become shipwrecked if they
do not wish to.

Caesar is regarded as the man who has robbed
the Romans of their freedom:

In the eyes of my enemies I sit clothed in liberties which
I have stolen from others. The word freedom is in everyone's mouth, though in the sense that it is being used no
one has ever been free or ever will be free . . . there is
no liberty save in responsibility. That I cannot rob them
of because they have not got it. . . . The Romans have
become skilled in the subtle resources for avoiding the
commitment and the price of political freedom. They
have become parasites upon that freedom which I gladly
exercise. . . .[6]

And he deals a passing blow at the Praetors Brutus
and Cassius, good clerks but his mortal enemies, who

". . . fulfill their duties with clerklike diligence; they mutter 'freedom, freedom,' " while pursuing nothing but their own narrow-minded ideas.

He, the dictator Julius Caesar, is not free. At the beginning of the first journal-letter to Turrinus he says: "I govern innumerable men but must acknowledge that I am governed by birds and thunderclaps."[7] A suffocating mass of superstitions sees in the entrails of birds, in their eating habits, in their flights, and in thunderstorms the daily augurs of the favor or disfavor of the gods. These superstitions impede all life, especially the operation of the state. The dictator seeks to restrain these malpractices; he would like to abolish them altogether. What is he to do?

He lists the things he has done. He has brought peace to the world; he has extended Roman law to innumerable men and women to whom he will also grant the rights of citizenship; he has reformed the calendar; he is arranging that the world be fed equably; he will abolish torture. "But these are not enough. . . . For the first time in my public life I am unsure."[8]

Caesar realizes that he must clear in his mind as to what are the aims in life of the average man and what one can expect of human nature. "Man—what is that? What do we know of him? His Gods, liberty, mind, love, destiny, death—what do these mean?"[9]

Of the traditional religious ideas he writes:

Even if we assume the existence of a God who, as Homer says, pours out from his urns his good and evil gifts, I am amazed at the pious who insult their God by failing to see that as this world is run there is a field of circumstance that is not commensurate with God's providence and that God must have so intended it.[10]

He tries to imagine what would happen if he abolished the gods. One night he actually draws up an edict abolishing the College of Augurs:

When have I been happier? What pleasures are greater than those of honesty? I wrote on and the constellations glided before my window. I disbanded the College of Vestal Virgins. . . . I closed the doors of the temples, of all our temples except those of Jupiter. I tumbled the gods back into the gulf of ignorance and fear from which they came and into that treacherous half-world where fancy invents consolatory lies. And finally the moment came when I pushed aside what I had done and started to begin again with the announcement that Jupiter himself had never existed; that man was alone in the world in which no voices were heard than his own, a world neither friendly nor unfriendly save as he made it so. And having reread what I wrote I destroyed it.[11]

But Caesar destroys what he has written not for reasons of state, for possible repercussions on the organization of the state, but because of something in himself:

Am I sure that there is no mind behind our existence and no mystery anywhere in the universe? . . . If that were so I could wish to live forever. How terrifying and glorious the role of man if, indeed, without guidance and without consolation he must create from his own vitals the meaning for his existence and write the rules whereby he lives.[12]

A final hesitation arrests his hand: he would have to be absolutely certain that in no corner of his being "there lingers the recognition that there is a possibility of mind in and behind the universe which influences our minds and shapes our actions."[13]

But there are four realms, he writes, in which he divines the possibility of this mystery in his life and in the life around him: in the erotic, in great poetry, in a transfiguring moment during an epileptic attack, and in a power beyond himself that seems to have shaped his life. "I seem to have known all my life, but to have refused to acknowledge that all, all love is one, and that the very mind with which I ask these questions is awakened, sustained, and instructed only by love."[14] And he goes on to say:

It may well be . . . that I am the most irresponsible of irresponsible men, capable long since of bringing upon Rome all the ills that a state can suffer, but for the fact that I was the instrument of a higher wisdom that selected me for my limitations and not for my strength. I do not reflect, and it may be that that instantaneous operation of my judgment is no other than the presence of the *daimon* within me, which is a stranger to me, and which is the love which the Gods bear to Rome. . . .[15]

Though it is quite improbable that Caesar ever sat at the deathbed of the poet Catullus or that he wrote down his reflections on death, Wilder's account is "true." In such passages as the following we may think of both Caesar and the one who wrote them: ". . . only those who have grasped their non-being are capable of praising the sunlight";[16] or: "I will

have no part in the doctrine of the stoics that the
contemplation of death teaches us the vanity of . . .
life's joys.";[17] or:

Oh, there are laws operating in the world whose import
we can scarcely guess. . . . At the close range we say
good and *evil*, but we are not present long enough to
glimpse more than two links in the chain. There lies the
regret at the brevity of life.[18]

This sovereign figure has behind him the experiences of Cardinal Vaini, the experiences of the five
victims of the collapsed bridge in Peru, the experiences of Pamphilus and Chrysis on the little island in
the Aegean, the experiences of Mr. Antrobus and of
Henry Antrobus. He also has known and understands
the life of Alcestis (whose story Catullus tells in part
at the dinner of Clodia), and he knows very well that
he will fall at the hands of a murderer.

This master of the world has also known "nothingness," though in a dream. "It is the state in which
one divines the end of all things. This nothingness,
however, does not present itself as a blank and a
quiet, but as a total evil unmasked."[19] But he also
knows the greatest happiness. In the paroxysm of his
illness comes such a moment: "I seem to grasp the
fair harmony of the world. . . . I wish to cry out to
all the living and the dead that there is no part of the
universe that is untouched by bliss."[20]

But it is not only in a dream that he has a vision
of evil nor only in his illness that he senses happiness. In a letter to Turrinus written a few weeks before his death Caesar writes:

. . . my waking state has been the contemplation of futility and the collapse of all belief. Oh, worse than that: my dead call me in mockery from their grave clothes and generations still unborn cry out, asking to be spared the clownish parade of mortal life. Yet even in my last bitterness I cannot disavow the memory of bliss. Life, life has this mystery that we dare not say the last word about it, that it is good or bad, that it is senseless, or that it is ordered. . . . the universe is not aware that we are here. . . . Life has no meaning save that which we confer upon it. . . . On the Meaningless I choose to press a meaning and in the wastes of the Unknowable I choose to be known.[21]

The mystery prevents him from "reaching a summary conclusion concerning our human condition. Where there is an Unknowable there is a promise."[22]

And then the dictator falls, a victim of the daggers of clerk souls, of theorists.

The Ides of March is an extraordinarily rich work. The abundance of life poured into this slight volume and the "truth" of the account are astonishing —an indication that mere accuracy does not determine the reality of truth; it resides in the self-contained cosmos of the work of art itself. And the central figure of this work of art, around which this cosmos revolves, is Caesar. The fact that this is Thornton Wilder's Caesar gives him, paradoxically, the appearance of objectivity, as though the historical Caesar could really have been like this.

10

The Alcestiad

*T*he *Ides of March* (1948) was followed two years later by "The Alcestiad" (published only in German as *Die Alkestiade,* 1960). In his search for a myth that had significance even for the present age, Wilder again turned to antiquity. To a dramatist, the mythical material of antiquity may seem more natural for an "abstract" drama than does a contemporary theme, which runs the risk of a treatment that may fall back on what Wilder considers "soothing" realism. And to transpose a myth of antiquity into the present, as O'Neill did in *Mourning Becomes Electra,* for example, may have seemed too problematical to Wilder. Be that as it may, in "The Alcestiad" Wilder chose a theme that was "ancient" even during the time of the classical tragedians. In fact it is a theme that Euripides (480–406 B.C.) treated.

This is the story of Alcestis, the Thessalian queen, wife of Admetus, whose husband is threatened by mortal danger and who offers to die in his stead. In Euripides's version, while the mourners are lamenting her death, Heracles passes through on his journey to King Diomedes whose man-eating horse he is to take to his master Eurystheus. Admetus does not tell his guest of Alcestis's death, but says the mourners are lamenting the death of a woman of the household. Heracles, drinking and singing, enjoys Admetus's famed hospitality, until he is apprised of the true situation. He reproaches his friend for his silence and hastens off to rescue Alcestis from Death. He succeeds and returns the woman to the disconsolate widower, who, incredulous at first, finally accepts his good fortune and leads home the wife he believed lost forever.

It is difficult not to feel some degree of contempt for Admetus for having accepted the sacrificial death of his wife and for having vainly requested this service of love from his father and mother. Wilder changes the myth radically: in his version, Admetus does not know the real reason for Alcestis's death, which makes the story much more acceptable to the modern reader.

Wilder divides the myth into three acts, which have little in common with the version of Euripides, although the first act begins, as does that of Euripides, with an expository dialogue between Apollo and Death. The god, smiling into the distance, announces to Death that a "change" has taken place, the beginning of a story that will teach even Death something. "Nothing will change," cries Death, an uncanny, waddling figure with bat wings, exemplifying the obstinate power of persistence.

The theme of the sacrificial death is presaged in this first act. King Admetus has won the right to Alcestis by accomplishing the task of harnessing a wild boar and a lion to a cart and driving this vehicle around Jolkos, the native city of Alcestis. On the night before her wedding Alcestis begs Apollo for a sign that her wish to serve him will be granted. "I want to live in the real," she says.

The seer Tiresias, an extremely old, blind choleric, and half-mad character, is announced. He foretells the appearance of four herdsmen, one of whom

will be Apollo. Here Wilder uses a motif from antiquity: Zeus has given Apollo the task of serving a
mortal being for a year, in order to expiate a killing.
(This same motif has appeared already in *The Cabala*,
where the gods in human form wander about among
mortals, unrecognized by them.) The four herdsmen
"conceal" the god whom Tiresias has announced: no
one knows which one of them is Apollo. The herdsman whom Alcestis questions even denies that one of
these unkempt, low characters could be the god. He
concedes, however, that the four, besides their very
ordinary, unsavory characteristics, are endowed with
remarkable gifts: one of them is a healer, another a
singer, the third has an unerring sense of direction.
But the herdsman assures Alcestis that there is no
god among them. While they are talking, Admetus,
the blue cloak—the sign of divinity—slung about his
shoulders, steps out of the palace.

Admetus tells Alcestis that she is free to leave
him, but he says quite simply that he loves her, and
for the love of her he accomplished the seemingly im-
possible. At this, she finally yields. She is now ready
to live for him and his children and his people, to live
for him as though she were willing at any moment to
die for him. Apollo (visible only to the audience),
overjoyed, hastens to the entrance of the underworld
and tells Death that he will teach him a lesson.

When Tiresias announced the four herdsmen, he
also prophesied a danger that was incomprehensible
to all. The danger now becomes apparent. The herdsman whom Alcestis questioned about Apollo quar-

rels with one of the others, draws a knife, and inadvertently injures the king. Admetus lies hopelessly languishing from the wound. Then comes the message from Delphi—a gold tablet on which is written that the king will live if someone is willing to die in his stead. The herdsman who inflicted the wound is willing; the night watchman is willing; the old servant Aglaia is willing. But Alcestis now sees an opportunity to fulfill her vow. She pledges the others to silence. Admetus knows nothing; he is surprised when he recovers his vitality and alarmed at Alcestis's increasing weakness. Alcestis dies, Heracles arrives, and the subsequent action is very much like that of the play's ancient prototype. It is told in a few sentences, and the drama would be over if Wilder had not added a third act that takes place twelve years later.

This act, like the first and second, begins at daybreak. Meanwhile there have been many changes. Instead of gentle Admetus, the barbarian King Agis of Thrace is now ruler. He has killed Admetus and two of his children and has driven Epimenides, the oldest son, out of the country. Alcestis, the former queen, is a slave at the king's court. A plague is raging in the land, and Alcestis is blamed for the epidemic. Scores of people are dying, and King Agis's daughter, Laodamia, has already succumbed. Again there is an altercation between Apollo and Death. Death is told by Apollo that he will be obliged to accept a change. Angrily, Death protests.

To King Agis, who is in despair over the death of his daughter, Alcestis says:

"Love is not the meaning. It is one of the signs that there is a meaning—it is only *one* of the signs that life has a meaning. For her, you see, it is death—despair. Her life remains vain and empty until you give it meaning."

What meaning could he, Agis, give life? Alcestis calmly tells him what a cruel and ignorant human being he is: "You killed *my* Laodamia. Three times. Senselessly. All the dead, King Agis, all those millions of dead implore us to prove that their lives were not empty and futile."

Epimenides, Admetus's son who was believed dead, appears with his friend Cheriander to take vengeance on Agis and his young daughter Laodamia for his father's death. Alcestis meets her son and makes herself known to him. She dissuades Epimenides from carrying out his revenge because of Agis's extreme unhappiness.

At the end of the play, Alcestis, after a final dialogue with Apollo, is staggering toward what she hopes and believes to be her grave, but the god promises her eternal life. "You are the first of a large number who will not have this end," he tells her. And when she asks to whom she is indebted for such happiness, he replies: "Friends do not ask one another that." Even after Alcestis has disappeared, Apollo calls after her: "Those who have loved do not ask one another that, Alcestis."

Alcestis is a saint and realizes what life means, not only "to a certain degree." Though she is a figure taken from prehistoric Greece, she is a saint of Christian characteristics. But she is one who does not, however, renounce earthly life after the manner of medieval Christianity. Aware that her suffering is not of the utmost, she says to her returned son: "Learn to recognize unhappiness when you see it. There is only one unhappiness and that is ignorance. . . . Not to know the meaning of our life. That is suffering and despair. . . ."

This play again has a certain sparseness of scenery, although the palace of Admetus, the courtyard gate, the entrance to the palace and to the servants' quarters are shown. In front of the footlights there is a path leading to a spring and to the shrub-encircled gate of the underworld from which Death emerges and into which Heracles disappears to rescue Alcestis. Apollo appears either in a gold cloak on the roof or, if the theater does not show the roof, he enters and leaves through the palace door, dressed in a long dark-blue hooded cloak meant to suggest his invisibility. In the last act he wears a gold laurel wreath. He is invisible to the rest of the characters of the play, with the exception of Death. Though he appears as a god, his role reminds one of the Stage Manager in *Our Town*. Apollo is the actual producer of this play, which is basically a confrontation between the god and Death.

To this gloomy, problematical drama Wilder added a satyr play, after the fashion of antiquity. It is called *The Drunken Sisters*, and in it Apollo tricks the Three Fates into giving him back the life of Admetus, who is already doomed. Disguised as a scullery boy, Apollo makes the three masked and rather

bored Parcaes (Atropos, Lachesis, and Voltho) drunk
with wine meant for Aphrodite. Since they promise
all kinds of things in their drunken state, he begs for
the life of Admetus. But they demand another life in
exchange; someone must offer himself voluntarily
for Admetus. "Oh!" Apollo cries, "now I see how it is
all coming out." And he calls: "Alcestis! Alcestis!"

The somewhat forced humor of this scene, which
does not end in the least humorously but quite grotesquely instead, fits the drama itself, which moves
without pathos along the extreme edge of the "unknowable." In view of Wilder's own aspirations, it is
understandable that he returned to Greek antiquity,
where the possibilities of the moral-ethical world
were discussed with passion, and the very borders of
the "unknowable" were approached in its tragedies.

11

Themes

Of all the unideological spirits of our disrupted age, Wilder is perhaps the least committed ideologically, the most "unlogical." He himself once said: "I have no ideas." He could be called a conservative spirit were it not that his novels and dramas were revolutionary in form. The existence of ideological endeavors to overcome human inadequacy by political collective systems has, up to now, been hardly acknowledged in Wilder's works, even in his dramatic ones. It is almost as though they did not exist. On the other hand, toward endeavors that were significant in the development of personality in the various cultures and religions throughout human history, especially in the Orient, Wilder has shown an extraordinary interest, indeed a passionate interest. But any convictions that he might have developed through this interest cannot be identified with any doctrine or discipline.

Wilder does not answer nor does he presume to be capable of answering the question of how one lives with any ideological formula. And this is actually the point of departure, the motif of his art. One might be inclined to assume that Wilder had written *The Woman of Andros* for the sake of Chrysis's doctrine and her story of the hero, or *Our Town* for the sake of Emily's experience of life and death. But though we believe it possible to assert that Pamphilus's question How does one live? is the guiding thought behind all Wilder's work, we must nevertheless keep in mind that his vital interest lay in the artistic shaping and grouping of the figures embodying that question.

When Wilder theorizes it is almost always about the problems of art. The purely conceptual problems that he expresses in his works are few compared to his images, and they leave no doubt of his artistic, rather than speculative, impulses. When asked in the Goldstone interview whether there were one or two ideas that ran through all his work, he replied that he thought there were, but that he had become aware of it only recently. "Now, at my age, I am amused by the circumstance that what is now conscious with me was for a long time latent."[1]

There is no reason to doubt this, though one might be tempted to single out the following passage from "The Angel That Troubled the Waters" as proof that the entire imagery had been invented to dramatize this "idea":

"Without your wound, where would your power be? It is your remorse that makes your low voice tremble into the hearts of men. The very angels themselves cannot persuade the wretched and blundering children on earth as can one human being broken on the wheels of living. In Love's service only the wounded soldiers can serve."[2]

The angel, however, is too concretely described in the play: "His face and robe shine with a color that is both silver and gold. And the wings of blue and green, tipped with rose, shimmer in the tremulous light."[3] One can say with some degree of certainty that this shining vision was primary, antecedent to the thoughts that the angel expresses. The rest of the scenery is also vividly described. It is certainly a structure of fantasy and, if translated into the reality of a production, would require a very complicated apparatus, especially with regard to lighting. What stimulated the author's imagination here was perhaps chiefly the visual element, the concrete experience, through which, to be sure, the idea becomes transparent. This is also true of the other youthful plays, such as "Leviathan" or "And the Sea Shall Give Up Its Dead."

Although Wilder's themes were perhaps not conscious ideas, the speeches of the angel, of the Fates in "Nascuntur Poetae," and of the Grey Steward (Death) in "Mozart and the Grey Steward" are actually messages containing ideas, and what the angel says to the sufferer is reminiscent of the Cardinal's words in *The Cabala*: "Who has not suffered . . ."

The ideas expressed in these messages may sound alien in our modern world. This is a peculiarity of Wilder's work that must strike everyone who studies it: the modern industrial, technological world has no place in Wilder's writing. More specifically, it has no influence on the consciousness of Wilder's characters, or only a very general, indirect influence insofar as the question How does one live? has received special emphasis in the present age. In the lives of the individual characters, at any rate, there is no question of such an influence, if only because most of them are at home in a preindustrial, pretechnological age. It is true that George Brush, the religious or pseudo-religious propagandist, lives in the America of the 1930s and uses the apparatus of its culture, but scarcely on a conscious level. His real and predominant interest is in the question of how one should live. He thinks he has found the answer, and machines are no part of it.

Mr. Antrobus invented the wheel and separated em from en in the alphabet. Though he takes pride in such civilizing achievements as beer-brewing and the invention of gunpowder, he does not seem to have placed the greatest value on them.

Although *The Skin of Our Teeth* comes very close to our present age with its catastrophes and the human consequences thereof—especially in the portrayal of Henry-Cain and his solipsistic nihilism— the aphorisms seem remote from the present. They originated in an age that could have had no conception of the revolution that altered the face of the world. Even Spinoza, whose "geometric" method is closer to us than the story of Adam and Eve, is not concerned with the industrial and technological revolution, for Spinoza's human being is one who has not yet been shaken by such a revolution.

How does one live? The question may not concern the man who draws oil from the ground or sends rockets into space. But the man who, under pressure of political terror, throttles his conscience; the man who realizes even in everyday life that on either side of life's narrow ledge he looks down into vertiginous abysses—this man can scarcely be saved by the rationality of technology, except perhaps in the challenge of the work it involves.

But even toward work Mr. Antrobus finds objections: "Work, work, work, that is all I do. I have ceased to live." What does this mean? Mr. Antrobus and his family have once again survived by the skin of their teeth; they can try to build a new world. The reference to certain maxims that constitute our spiritual heritage is meant to point out that man was never satisfied merely to cover his material needs. Though his material concern is vital and requires industry and organizing talent, yet from the moment man began ornamenting a clay pot, from the moment he lamented his dead in tones that gave him a vague inkling of music, from the very day he gazed reflectively into the fire he had kindled to render his food palatable, from the time he decided to see the sign of power in a crude clay figure—from these moments man began the difficult and involved task of building a world of his own, always knowing when he came up against a boundary that something boundless lay beyond.

A motif that is mentioned again and again, especially in the early works, is the one of the dual reality, as Death expresses it in the Mozart play. This contrast is present in the world of Wilder's earliest fancies. A further motif was added: only the sufferer is destined to see the reality that lies behind or within actuality, and only he can give it perceptual form, for the sake of the millions who are unable to do so. The boy in "Nascuntur Poetae" is taught: "Others shall know a certain peace and shall live well enough in the limits of life they know; . . . For you there shall be ever beyond the present a lost meaning and a more meaningful love."[4] This is the suffering to which the angel that troubles the waters refers: "In Love's service only the wounded soldier can serve."[5] Hosts of angels are not able to do what a single human being can do "who has been broken on the wheels of living."

It is obvious that basically all these plays have a religious, more specifically, a Christian content. But Wilder does not commit himself. For him, even in the earliest works, religion is not a doctrine, not an "idea" or abstraction that, paradoxically linked with actual existence, burdens common sense with conflicting enigmas. One might almost say that religion for him is something perceptively tangible, though beyond the here and now. It is life that is accessible perhaps only to the imagination, but once revealed, it is seen to be meaningful and significant.

Wilder demonstrated this view of religion in images; for example, in the figure of the donkey Hepzibah who carries the Mother of God on the flight into Egypt and keeps standing still because she is tired or because she feels like discussing the relationship of faith and reason. Or it can be seen in the figure of the servant Malchus, who thinks he has been made to look ridiculous.

Other themes bound up with the "things that lie beyond the present" are the theme of permanence or eternity and that of limitless time and space. The latter determines the form of "The Long Christmas Dinner," in which a family sits at an endless meal

throughout generations. In "Pullman Car Hiawatha," though the train is en route from New York
to Chicago on a certain date, the human experiences
that take place are seen as universal experiences.

These experiences beyond time and space, which
are accessible only to the imagination but out of
which human beings fashion their world, dominate
Wilder's work. They can also lead to a certain buf-
foonery growing out of delusions, as in "Queens of
France." Here several more or less respectable
middle-class women of New Orleans are deluded by
an uncanny, fraudulent lawyer into believing that
they are legitimate heirs of the Bourbons and pre-
tenders to the throne of France.

This delusion is treated as comedy in "Queens of
France," but for the characters in *The Cabala* the
nonexistent dream world becomes tragic and destroys
them. The most distinguished among them, the Cardinal, destroys even this dream world of the other
members, and his skepticism destroys his own world,
which his faith had built. From Sophocles's *Oedipus
at Colonus*, the Cardinal cites the passage about the
confusion of all-mastering time: "The strength of
earth decays and the strength of the body. Faith dies.
Distrust is born. Among friends the same spirit does
not last true. . . ."[6] Yet man goes on longing for the
world that lies beyond the present.

This longing will ultimately remain unfulfilled
if the theme is rooted in death. In *The Bridge of San
Luis Rey*, Father Juniper was unable to discover the
intentions of Providence. "The longer he worked the

more he felt that he was stumbling about among great dim intimations."[7] The very essence of the mystery is its inability to be clarified.

The theme of "things that lie beyond the present" is expanded and deepened by yet another element: the element of love. The characters in Wilder's early works, in *The Cabala, The Bridge of San Luis Rey,* and *The Woman of Andros,* live outside the family or in a family relationship of tension. Yet they are all directly or indirectly concerned with love, with a love that is unfulfilled in a worldly sense. "Who can understand love unless he has loved without response?" This understanding is shared by the Marquesa de Montemayor, by Uncle Pio, by the hetaera Chrysis, and by the Princess d'Espoli. And perhaps the most pitiable in his need for love is Esteban, who, after the loss of his twin brother, loses his own identity, and in his despair seeks death. "I am alone, alone, alone," he cries. He is in extreme contrast to Henry-Cain, who believes that he can find his being's ultimate fulfillment in aloneness. But they are all aware of what love is or can be: ". . . the bridge between the land of the living and the land of the dead . . . the only survival, the only meaning."[8]

In his early works, up through *The Bridge of San Luis Rey,* Wilder draws a wide arc: from the hetaera Chrysis to the Christian Abbess María del Pilar, from priestlike Pamphilus to suicidal Esteban, from the mad sea captain Philocles in *The Woman of Andros* to Captain Alvarado in *The Bridge of San Luis Rey.* There is something extreme in the behavior of these people, a demand for the absolute. This is present in Henry Antrobus's wish to be alone and in Esteban's despair over the loss of his brother, his mirror image. There is something extreme in the suggestion that Jesus is "ridiculous," that is, in the alternative suggested: either the Nazarene was a fool or he created a new and definitive norm of what is human. And suffering derives from the fact that no one is able to conform to this norm; to recognize the norm as compulsive means to suffer.

For those characters who long to live in "reality,"—a trait of self-destruction, or rather self-abnegation, drives them into the very heart of suffering, which is at the same time the core of the individual, the personality—of Alcestis or Pamphilus, for example. And at this point the theme passes over into the general; their suffering speaks for the millions who cannot give expression to their dull pain save in a cry of despair.

The actress Perichole, who has given up acting and, to a certain extent, the world itself, stands before Uncle Pio who loves her, who wishes to educate her son. "Her eyes were resting on the star that seemed to be leading forth the whole sky in its wonder. A great pain lay at her heart, the pain of a world that was meaningless."[9] Meaningless—even for those who have found a certain measure of peace and contentment within the boundaries of life. For, roused from this peace by death, like the hero in the story Chrysis tells, and like Emily in *Our Town,* they look back into the life they have lived and realize that the living do not understand this life; only the saints and poets do, to some extent. Nevertheless, this earthly, imperfect life, devoid of all penetrating love, is not ascetically renounced.

Between the affirmation of earthly life and the difficulty or impossibility of ever fully understanding it there is a wide gap that perhaps reaches its extreme in the "Alcestiad." Alcestis wishes to serve her god in order to live in "reality"—she wishes to merge with the divine. She disavows earthly life, but later, through great happiness and intense suffering, the god whom she wishes to serve shows her that even love is not the meaning of life. Thus she spans the widest arc of all the Wilder figures.

In all these works of Wilder, the religious question How does one live? is never formulated as a theory. If there is something absolute by which human beings can orient their lives, it is neither the state nor society nor the rationale of technology. All these authorities have their limits beyond which questions such as the relation of the individual to the universal become crucial.

We cannot ignore the theme of the future. Thornton Wilder's work, in an immaterial sense, contains the man of the twentieth century who, in the maelstrom of toppling orders, has frighteningly lost his orientation. Faced with the question of how to live, what is left for him but to trust, like Caesar, the promise that grows out of the unknowable?

Postscript

The Eighth Day (1967), Wilder's most recent novel, is the longest of any of his works to date. There is a twelve-year span between this novel and the Edinburgh production of his last play, "A Life in the Sun." And almost twenty years separate *The Eighth Day* from the preceding novel, *The Ides of March.*

The Eighth Day received mixed reviews from the critics on its appearance. One reviewer had a comment to make on the unusual length of a Wilder work: ". . . where Wilder's prose was honed to succinct statements of affirmation in the past, it is now lengthened and pedantic. His lyrical qualities are diffused, his plot ambiguous and his theme labyrinthine."[1] But, almost a contradiction, Malcolm Cowley wrote in *Book Week*: "Wilder has a way of choosing the necessary facts and of stating them in the simplest and briefest fashion. The facts may be prosaic, but his statements are as hard to change as a finished line of poetry."[2]

The formal structure of *The Eighth Day* is more conventional than that of *The Ides of March*, since it is a narration with considerable dialogue. The narrator takes much the same position as the Stage Manager in *Our Town* in that he assumes the role of the prescient observer. But of more significance, perhaps, is the kind of narrative technique used by Wilder throughout *The Eighth Day*: the narrator is not only aware of the future of the characters, but he also inserts maxims into the story line and makes comparisons between the particular and the universal. This vision of the whole stems more from Wilder than from the characters themselves. Helmut Papajewski suggests that Wilder's use of this technique makes him into one

who knows more than they [the characters] do, even if he does not "know better" than they. In contrast to the writers of many other auctorial novels, he avoids a conservatism that would cause him to stand out in contrast to his characters. In this way his narrative technique and his narrative content become in a sense harmonized.[3]

With *The Eighth Day*, Wilder once again returned to an American setting and to the early twentieth century. The narration is concerned essentially with the three years 1902–1905, but chapters one, four, and five take the reader back as far as 1880 and bring him through the years to 1905 again. The future is introduced, by the prescient narrator, in the Prologue and in a kind of epilogue in the last chapter, as well as in insertions throughout the body of the novel—many of these being treated almost like an aside.

The Prologue, "calculated to amaze the reader—but a beginning that wins the reader by its humor, irony, and self-irony,"[4] serves a number of purposes. The reader becomes aware in the first paragraphs that this will be a kind of mystery novel:

In the early summer of 1902 John Barrington Ashley of Coaltown, a small mining center in southern Illinois, was tried for the murder of Breckenridge Lansing, also of Coaltown. He was found guilty and sentenced to death. Five days later, at one in the morning of Tuesday, July 22, he escaped from his guards on the train that was carrying him to his execution.

. . . About five years later, the State's Attorney's office in Springfield announced that fresh evidence had been uncovered fully establishing Ashley's innocence.[5]

Thus, it is left to the rest of the novel to disclose who actually did murder Breckenridge Lansing and who the mysterious, silent, unarmed rescuers of Ashley were. But in actuality, the novel is little concerned with the "mystery case." Of greater importance are the intertwining lives of the Ashley and Lansing families—in particular, the children and John Ashley—and their histories in relation to the history of mankind, a history that is *"one* tapestry" and of which "no eye can venture to compass more than a hand's-breadth."[6]

This idea of family histories in relation to the whole is immediately set forth in the Prologue after the brief discussion of the "Ashley case." The characteristics of the Ashley children, who are likened to their father, are described from the vantage point of their future achievements—Roger was to become a very famous journalist, Lily a celebrated singer, and

Constance an internationally known social reformer.
The reader is told that as early as 1910 "people began . . . to ask questions—frivolous or thoughtful
questions—about John and Beata Ashley and their
children, about Coaltown, about those old teasers
Heredity and Environment, about gifts and talents,
about destiny and chance."[7] At this point one of the
more obvious themes in Wilder's works becomes apparent: "Was there a connection between the catastrophe that befell both houses and these later devel-
opments? Are humiliation, injustice, suffering, desti-
tution, and ostracism—are they blessings?"[8]

But the reader is introduced not only to the two
families in relation to history, but to Coaltown and
many of its inhabitants as well. After a brief description of Coaltown in 1902, a background of the town
and surrounding area is given. This is not just a conventional background to familiarize the reader with
the setting, but a history that encompasses the evolu-
tion of the plants and animals, the production of coal
from the forests, and finally the coming of man and
the history of the Kangaheela Indian tribe. Wilder
goes even further; he foreshadows Coaltown's future,
where it is seen quite differently than it is in
1902–1905.

The Prologue serves yet another purpose. It is
here that the meaning of the title is disclosed. Dr.
Gillies, the town's "most articulate and exasperating
philosopher," gives an impromptu speech at the New
Year's Eve gathering, 1899. The Creation, which, according to the Bible, took six days—each day lasting

millions of years—was not finished with God's creating man. On the seventh day God rested, but now, in 1900, man is beginning a new week, and the Creation will continue:

"In this new century we shall be able to see that mankind is entering a new stage of development—the Man of the Eighth Day. . . . Mind and Spirit will be the next climate of the human. The race is undergoing its education. What is education, Roger? What is education, George? It is the bridge man crosses from the self-enclosed, self-favoring life into a consciousness of the entire community of man."[9]

In this speech Wilder displays a great deal of irony, for Dr. Gillies himself believes nothing he says. His real expectation is that this century will be as disastrous as any other. He cannot see that there had ever been Golden Ages or Dark Ages; only the same monotony operating under fair and foul weather. But, nevertheless, he continues for the sake of the young people present: "It is the duty of old men to lie to the young. Let these encounter their own disillusions. We strengthen our souls, when young, on hope; the strength we acquire enables us later to endure despair as a Roman should."[10]

The actual present of the novel can be considered as beginning in 1902 after Ashley's mysterious escape. It then carries the reader through the events between this time and Christmas 1905, when Roger Ashley discovers that it was George Lansing who murdered his own father—to keep worse things from happening—and that the group of men who rescued

Ashley were from a small religious sect—a religious sect to which Ashley did not belong but whom he had once helped to build a church after a disaster.

The Ashley family, surrounded by the gossip and sneers of a small-town environment, are faced with finding a means of livelihood. Roger, the seventeen-year-old son, leaves for Chicago, where he assumes another name and holds several jobs before becoming a journalist. Lily, the oldest daughter, remains in Coaltown for a time, and then also goes to Chicago. An entire chapter is set in this city and devoted to telling the story of Roger's and Lily's development—both "late-maturing and little given to reflection" like their father.

It is fourteen-year-old Sophia Ashley who discovers and utilizes resources for the family's livelihood—usually against her mother's will. Through her efforts "The Elms," the home of the Ashleys, is converted into a boardinghouse, whereby Mrs. Ashley is forced out of her self-imposed seclusion. Perhaps Wilder is making a definite contrast between Sophia and the three other Ashley children. Sophia is forced to mature early, while Lily, Roger, and Constance are allowed to be "late-maturing." But Sophia is the only one of the Ashley children who does not later become famous—who, indeed, becomes insane.

The second chapter follows John Ashley, in his various disguises and under several aliases, to New Orleans and finally to Chile, where he works in the Rocas Verdes copper mines. It is during this journey and Ashley's sojourn in Chile that Wilder takes the opportunity to draw the characteristics of a "man of faith."

John Ashley was a man of faith. He did not know that he was a man of faith. He would have been quick to deny that he was a man of religious faith, but religions are merely the garments of faith. . . .

There is no faith and hope that does not express itself in creation. These men and women work. . . . This work that they do may often seem to be all but imperceptible. That is characteristic of activity that never for a moment envisages an audience.[11]

Ashley is further described to the reader as a man with a certain sureness, though he lacks those traits that "engage interest"—aggression, dominating will, destructiveness and self-destructiveness—traits of a Breckenridge Lansing, for instance. Perhaps Wilder's repeated reference to John Ashley as "late-maturing" is used with irony, or perhaps it is meant to describe that quality in Ashley that comes from a complete lack of self-awareness.

It is conceivable that it was this chapter dealing with John Ashley that prompted Granville Hicks to write in the *Saturday Review*:

Wilder's way of commenting on the characters does not diminish one's sense of their reality but enhances it. In fact, he seems more objective than the impersonal moderns, for he talks about these people as if they were real. . . . [He] offers the reader no certainty, but he does inspire a beautiful sense of human possibilities. He does not deny the existence of evil . . . but he believes that for some people in some places in some times life can be satisfying.[12]

This last statement would certainly seem to apply to Ashley as he is seen in this chapter. The reader senses that Ashley is a man who has little trouble finding satisfaction whatever his circumstances.

Just as Ashley built a church for the religious sect near Coaltown, in Chile he builds a Catholic chapel for the mineworkers. He meets and develops a strong friendship with Mrs. Wickersham, the founder of. an orphanage and hospital in Manantiales, Chile. She, too, is one of these people of faith. It is through her contrivance that Ashley manages to escape capture by a man who has recognized him. Wilder ends this episode just as imperturbably as he did those in *The Bridge of San Luis Rey*. Mrs. Wickersham receives a letter from Ashley twelve days after his Chilean escape. "Several weeks later she received another by slow coastal mail. He was leaving Tiburones the next day for the north. She received no more. He was drowned at sea."[13]

Chapter four is treated as a flashback into family history. The reader is reintroduced to John and Beata Ashley during their courtship in Hoboken, New Jersey. Beata's German background is discussed to some length, as each of her characteristics are shown to be tied to either her mother's or her father's family. And here the reader is also introduced to the circumstances surrounding the "marriage" of John and Beata.

Not until chapter five is a complete picture of the Lansing family offered. This is treated, like chapter four, as a flashback into family history, this time those of Breckenridge Lansing and his wife, Eustacia. The twenty-five years from 1880 to 1905 are spanned without interruption. Breckenridge Lansing's attempts to establish a patriarchal home—characterized, in his eyes, by contempt for wife and family—only lead to complete alienation of his son, George. For the first time, the reader becomes familiar with George and his sister Félicité, with whom George is able to form his only stable relationship, excepting that with John Ashley. And, to a lesser extent, tantrum-inclined Anne, the youngest of the Lansing children and her father's favorite, is introduced into the novel.

This chapter, which reiterates in detail the events leading to Breckenridge Lansing's murder, consists in large part of letters between Félicité and George, who supposedly had left home the night before his father's death. George's character is more fully revealed through these letters.

It is left to the relatively short final chapter to disclose the "mystery" details. But here Wilder also takes the opportunity to expound on his theories of the history of mankind. He attempts, through his narrator, to clarify the concepts of history and time.

This is a history.

But there is only one history. It began with the creation of man and will come to an end when the last human consciousness is extinguished. All other beginnings and endings are arbitrary conventions. . . .

It is only in appearance that time is a river. It is rather a vast landscape and it is the eye of the beholder that moves.[14]

The reader is finally allowed a more detailed glimpse into the future lives of the novel's characters in this epiloguelike chapter. He now sees these events, however, as they apply to the continuation of this one and only history. Wilder's is a very visual concept. The closing paragraph and especially the final sentence, which is followed by no punctuation, clearly show that Wilder means to leave the question of the existence of a design in this "tapestry" an open one.

There is much talk of a design in the arras. Some are certain they see it. Some see what they have been told to see. Some remember that they saw it once but have lost it. Some are strengthened by seeing a pattern wherein the oppressed and exploited of the earth are gradually emerging from their bondage. Some find strength in the conviction that there is nothing to see. Some[15]

Notes

Chapter 1: *Anonymous, but Not Impersonal*

1. *Writers at Work: The Paris Review Interviews,* ed. with introduction by Malcolm Cowley, New York: Viking Press, 1958, p. 103
2. *Loc. cit.*
3. *Ibid.,* p. 107
4. *Ibid.,* p. 108
5. *Ibid.,* p. 107
6. Thornton Wilder, *Three Plays,* New York: Bantam Books, 1958, p. xii
7. *Writers at Work,* p. 116
8. *Loc. cit.*
9. *Ibid.,* p. 117
10. *Ibid.,* p. 105

Chapter 2: *The Cabala*

1. Thornton Wilder, *The Cabala,* New York: Albert and Charles Boni, 1928, p. 49
2. *Ibid.,* p. 187
3. *Ibid.,* p. 225
4. *Ibid.,* p. 229

Chapter 3: *The Bridge of San Luis Rey*

1. Thornton Wilder, *The Bridge of San Luis Rey,* New York: Albert and Charles Boni, 1928, p. 15

2.   *Ibid.,* p. 139
3.   *Ibid.,* p. 190
4.   *Ibid.,* p. 204
5.   *Ibid.,* p. 52
6.   *Ibid.,* p. 36
7.   *Ibid.,* pp. 85ff.

Chapter 4: Three-Minute Plays

1.   Thornton Wilder, *The Angel That Troubled the Waters,* New York: Coward-McCann, 1928, p. 124
2.   *Loc. cit.*
3.   *Ibid.,* pp. 86ff.
4.   *Ibid.,* p. 87
5.   *Ibid.,* p. 83
6.   *Ibid.,* p. 99
7.   *Ibid.,* p. 102
8.   *Ibid.,* p. 103
9.   *Ibid.,* p. 140
10. *Ibid.,* p. 112
11. *Ibid.,* p. 131
12. *Ibid.,* p. 133
13. *Loc. cit.*

Chapter 5: The Woman of Andros

1.   Thornton Wilder, *The Woman of Andros,* New York: Albert and Charles Boni, 1930, p. 36
2.   *Ibid.,* p. 37
3.   *Ibid.,* p. 38
4.   *Ibid.,* p. 37
5.   *Ibid.,* p. 184
6.   *Ibid.,* p. 160
7.   *Ibid.,* p. 181
8.   *Ibid.,* pp. 197ff.

9.   *Ibid.*, p. 198
10. *Ibid.*, p. 203
11. *Ibid.*, p. 62
12. *Ibid.*, p. 7
13. *Ibid.*, p. 162

Chapter 6: One-Act Plays

1.   Thornton Wilder, *The Long Christmas Dinner*, New York: Coward-McCann, Yale University Press, 1931, p. 1
2.   *The Long Christmas Dinner*, New York: Harper Colophon, 1964, p. 3
3.   *The Long Christmas Dinner*, New York: Coward-McCann, Yale University Press, p. 27
4.   *Ibid.*, p. 63

Chapter 7: Heaven's My Destination

1.   Thornton Wilder, *Heaven's My Destination*, New York: Harper & Row, 1935, p. 146
2.   *Ibid.*, p. 148
3.   *Ibid.*, p. 294
4.   *Ibid.*, p. 300
5.   *Ibid.*, p. 151
6.   *Ibid.*, p. 304

Chapter 8: Three Plays

1.   Thornton Wilder, *Three Plays*, New York: Bantam Books, 1958, p. vii
2.   *Ibid.*, p. viii
3.   *Ibid.*, p. xi

4.   Thornton Wilder, *Our Town*, New York: Coward McCann Inc., 1938, p. 9
5.   *Ibid.*, p. 13
6.   *Ibid.*, p. 128
7.   *Three Plays*, p. xi
8.   *Our Town*, p. 54
9.   *Ibid.*, p. 124
10. *Ibid.*, p. 125
11. *Loc. cit.*
12. Thornton Wilder, *The Skin of Our Teeth*, New York: Harper & Brothers, 1942, p. 84
13. *Ibid.*, p. 100
14. *Ibid.*, p. 103
15. *Ibid.*, p. 130
16. *Loc. cit.*
17. *Loc. cit.*
18. *Loc. cit.*
19. *Ibid.*, pp. 130ff.
20. *Ibid.*, p. 132
21. *Loc. cit.*
22. *Ibid.*, p. 135
23. *Ibid.*, p. 136
24. *Ibid.*, p. 142
25. *Three Plays*, p. xi
26. *Ibid.*, pp. 224–25

Chapter 9: The Ides of March

1.   Thornton Wilder, *The Ides of March*, New York: Harper & Brothers, 1948, p. viii
2.   Helmut Papajewski, *Thornton Wilder*, New York: Frederick Ungar, 1968, p. 62
3.   *The Ides of March*, p. vii
4.   *Ibid.*, p. v
5.   *Ibid.*, p. 14
6.   *Ibid.*, pp. 237ff.

7. *Ibid.*, p. 5
8. *Ibid.*, pp. 7ff.
9. *Ibid.*, p. 8
10. *Ibid.*, p. 16
11. *Ibid.*, p. 37
12. *Loc. cit.*
13. *Ibid.*, p. 38
14. *Ibid.*, p. 39
15. *Ibid.*, pp. 39ff.
16. *Ibid.*, p. 184
17. *Loc. cit.*
18. *Ibid.*, p. 185
19. *Ibid.*, p. 231
20. *Loc. cit.*
21. *Ibid.*, pp. 232ff.
22. *Ibid.*, p. 239

Chapter 11: Themes

1. *Writers at Work*, p. 112
2. *The Angel That Troubled the Waters*, p. 149
3. *Ibid.*, p. 145
4. *Ibid.*, p. 122
5. *Ibid.*, p. 149
6. *The Cabala*, p. 204
7. *The Bridge of San Luis Rey*, p. 217
8. *Ibid.*, p. 235
9. *Ibid.*, p. 204

Postscript: The Eighth Day

1. On *The Eighth Day—Time*, 31 March 1967, p. 96
2. Malcolm Cowley, on *The Eighth Day—Book Week*,
    2 April 1967, p. 1
3. Helmut Papajewski, *Thornton Wilder*, pp. 191–92

4.   *Ibid.*, p. 178
5.   Thornton Wilder, *The Eighth Day*, New York: Harper & Row, 1967, p. 3
6.   *Ibid.*, p. 435
7.   *Ibid.*, p. 10
8.   *Loc. cit.*
9.   *Ibid.*, pp. 17–18
10. *Ibid.*, p. 18
11. *Ibid.*, pp. 106, 107
12. Granville Hicks, on *The Eighth Day—Saturday Review*, 1 April 1967, p. 25
13. *Ibid.*, p. 203
14. *Ibid.*, p. 395
15. *Ibid.*, p. 435

Chronology

1897: Thornton Wilder was born 17 April in Madison, Wisconsin.

1911/12: Lived in China and was a pupil in an English and a German mission school.

1915: Graduated from Berkeley High School, Berkeley, California.

1915–17: Studied at Oberlin College, Oberlin, Ohio.

1918: Studied at Yale University and served eight months in the coast artillery.

1920: Received a Bachelor of Arts degree from Yale University. His first play, *The Trumpet Shall Sound*, appeared in a magazine.

1920/21: Studied archaeology at the American Academy in Rome.

1922–24: Taught French in Lawrenceville, New Jersey.

1925: Received the degree of Master of Arts.

1927: Received the Pulitzer Prize for *The Bridge of San Luis Rey*.

1938: Awarded the Pulitzer Prize for *Our Town*.

1942–45: Military service, as captain and later as lieutenant colonel, in Africa and Italy. World premiere of *The Skin of Our Teeth*. Awarded the Pulitzer Prize for *The Skin of Our Teeth*.

1950/51: Professorship at Harvard.

1952: Headed the American delegation at the UNESCO conference in Venice.

1955: "A Life in the Sun" and *The Matchmaker* were performed at the Edinburgh Festival.

1957: Awarded the Peace Prize of the German Book Trade, the Goethe Plaque, and the Peace Medal of Pour le Merité.

1961: Performance of "The Long Christmas Dinner" in Mannheim, Germany.

1962: Performance of "The Alcestiad" as an opera (by Louise Talma) in Frankfurt-on-the-Main, Germany.

Bibliography

Works by Thornton Wilder

The Cabala, novel (1926)

The Bridge of San Luis Rey, novel (1927)

The Angel That Troubled the Waters: Three-Minute Plays for Three People (1928; includes: "Nascuntur Poetae. . . ," "Proserpine and the Devil," "Brother Fire," "Childe Roland to the Dark Tower Came," "The Angel on the Ship," "Centaurs," "Leviathan," "And the Sea Shall Give Up Its Dead," "Now the Servant's Name Was Malchus," "Mozart and the Grey Steward," "Hast Thou Considered My Servant Job?," "Flight Into Egypt," "The Angel That Troubled the Waters")

The Woman of Andros, novel (1930)

The Long Christmas Dinner, and Other Plays in One Act (1931; includes: "The Happy Journey To Trenton and Camden," "The Long Christmas Dinner," "Love and How to Cure It," "Pullman Car Hiawatha")

Our Town, play (1935)

The Merchant of Yonkers, play (1939; republished as *The Matchmaker*, 1957)

The Skin of Our Teeth, play (1942)

The Ides of March, novel (1948)

Three Plays (1957; includes: *Our Town, The Skin of Our Teeth, The Matchmaker*)
Die Alkestiade, with Satyr Play *Die beschwipsten Schwestern* (1960; German version of unpublished *A Life in the Sun* and *The Drunken Sisters*)
The Eighth Day, novel (1967)

Selected Works about Thornton Wilder

Brown, E. K. "A Christian Humanist." *University of Toronto Quarterly*, April 1935.
Burbank, Rex. *Thornton Wilder*. 1961.
Campbell, Joseph, and Robinson, H. M. "The Skin of Whose Teeth?" *Saturday Review of Literature*, 19 December 1942, 13 February 1943.
Edelstein, J. M. *A Bibliographical Checklist of the Writings of Thornton Wilder*. 1959.
Fergusson, Francis. "Three Allegorists: Brecht, Wilder and Eliot." *Sewanee Review*, 1956.
Firebaugh, Joseph J. "The Humanism of Thornton Wilder." *Pacific Spectator*, Fall 1950.
Fuller, Edmund. "Thornton Wilder: The Notation of a Heart." *American Scholar*, Spring 1959.
Goldstein, Malcolm L. *Art of Thornton Wilder*. 1965.
Grebanier, Bernard. *Thornton Wilder*. 1964.
Guthrie, Tyrone. "The World of Thornton Wilder." *The New York Times Magazine*, 27 November 1955.
Habermann, Donald. *Plays of Thornton Wilder: A Critical Study*. 1967.
Hamburger, Käte. *From Sophocles to Sartre: Figures from Greek Tragedy, Classical and Modern*. 1969.
Kohler, David. "Thornton Wilder." *The English Journal*, 1939.
Papajewski, Helmut. *Thornton Wilder*. 1968.
Szondi, Peter. *Theorie des modernen Dramas*. 1956.

Index